Good Things Happened Today

Good Things Happened Today

Christopher Atwood

ISBN 978-1-4357-6699-0

Prologue

Reverend Martin Luther King once urged us, "Put yourself in a state of mind where you say to yourself, 'Here is an opportunity for me to celebrate like never before, my own power, my own ability to get myself to do whatever is necessary.'"

Out of context, there is no meaning to his words. Fully internalized and fully realized, these words are some of the most powerful that were ever conceived.

Critical thought creates meaningful words, and words are our doorway to action. Action is our doorway to change. I was once jaded by my own judgments, imprisoned by thoughts, prejudices, and feelings that were not necessarily mine. Ironically, thoughts can be your own worst enemy or possibly your doorway to transformation and salvation. It can be done. It's just up to you. "I" could be you, if you wanted "I" to be you.

I love you guys … and I am always thinking about you. Always.

Chapter 1

What's in it for me? Who would want to start every conversation with those words? I did. Not literally, of course, but figurative imagination runs deep.

I thought about no one as I crossed those cold, brutal, and utterly exhilarating New York City streets. A carnivore with cognitive capabilities in perpetual motion, I was off to work, off to a meeting, off to dinner, off to extend my reach among the social elite. And I was always off to a place where my real thoughts were crowded out by impulse and stimulation. I stomped manically through my life like a thoughtless dolt through his father's prized flowers. And as I stomped over those in my path, I was being catapulted catatonically through the world around me.

Sure, I had lots of friends and family, even an ex-wife that used to love me very much. I chastised her jealously one New Year's Eve without ever recognizing her insecurity and rage over my own megalomania. She cried. I pressed hard. She flew out into the harsh, freezing New York night. I stayed working two or three more bourbons before the harsh, freezing reality set in. Our separation hurt for awhile, mostly because it was beyond my control, but nobody was as important as me or my ability to make money, and I was soon over it.

Anyway, the kill was exhilarating, but the meal was always … well, ordinary. I had to conquer it, and I was on my way. There was nothing—and no one—that deserved more thought or money than … well, me.

It's not fair to say I *never* thought about my life as it related to others. I did catch glimpses of who I used to be, or more accurately, who I would become. But those thoughts were fleeting. Pretty pathetic. The time I spent thinking about my life and its meaning to others equaled a step off the curb, a raised hand, and a loud yell of, "Taxi!" And that step down onto the bitter, dirty street, still a bit slippery from the late winter cold, was analogous in many ways to where I was in my own spiritual journey. But off I went, once again "clean" and "focused," off to arrest my mind with the inane cacophony that was my life.

So where did my coveted megalomania take me? It wrapped me in a warm, insulated feeling of superiority and control for years, driving me to make more money, more friends, more power ... more of anything related to me. But before I knew what happened, I had a labyrinth of thoughts that kept me focused on the idols in front of me, not the people around me, and certainly not the true reflection of my own soul and that which filled it with life. The tighter I squeezed my self-importance, the harder I ran from my life's true meaning, causing my mind to become crowded with negative predications of pain, death, and despair. But I never saw the correlation. I was on top of the world, yet I was empty and alone, questioning my own existence. In fact, most days, I was just a breath away from crying. Do you know what I mean? Slowly, quietly, I was being executed by my own thoughts. Thank God he gave us resilience and choice. "Taxi!"

For those reasons, among a lifetime of others, I awoke that Monday morning in March—as I did for the 5,210 days before—at 5:14 AM sharp with the smell of cappuccino floating into the bedroom of my upper west side apartment. Don't ask me why I set my alarm clock at exactly fourteen minutes past five because I don't know. Maybe it was because I always wore the number fourteen on my baseball jersey growing up. Or maybe I did it because fourteen was my favorite number. And I couldn't tell you whether it was the number I wore on my baseball jersey because it was my favorite number or vice versa. I always thought magical things happened at fourteen past the hour. It didn't matter; there was never a bit of deviation from the sequence.

Outside, there were familiar noises: an occasional dog barked, a faint car alarm sounded in the distance, intermittent honking. The City was just starting to stir, and I was getting ready to join its choreographed monotony for reasons I never resisted, even though they asphyxiated my proper place in the world. I never reflected long enough to understand why I routinely awoke in a city I did not necessarily like to go to a job that did not necessarily fulfill me in order to blatantly ignore the chance to fill my life with meaningful experiences—and that chance was evaporating as fast as my own life passed. For some reason, the sequence was too important.

There was light in my life. I loved my apartment. It was located on West 70th Street, just off Central Park West and only steps away from "The Park." Located on the top floor of an authenticate four-story brownstone built in 1890, it consisted of a little more than twelve hundred square feet, but much of its original high quality Victorian detailing had been beautifully preserved. My front door opened into what used to be the old, grand living room, with the original cornice molding circling the ceiling that loomed twelve-and-a-half feet above the finely restored original wide plank red oak floors. Those floors had been restored many times over the years, but they were gorgeous and still saturated with their original high society elegance and contempt. There were certain areas of the wood that were uneven, especially in places where the timber met the exposed brick on the east wall, but an ornate marble fireplace masked these imperfections.

My kitchen, like most of the modest furnishings found throughout, was modern but comfortable. I had opened the space up entirely; only an island bar separated the grand living room from the granite counters, cherry cabinets, and stainless steel appliances that adorned my kitchen. I even had a large ceramic hood installed over my professional-grade stove and range. It looked amazing, and most importantly, it impressed people. More than the refined appointments or original hardwood floors, the hood impressed people. And I loved getting lost in my cooking, lost in myself, particularly after a half dozen bourbons paved the way.

The wrought iron railing, maintained from the original house overlooking the stairwell, was now enclosed in my home and acted as a guide leading along the outward wall down the hallway, straight toward a closet. An assortment of original Chigal sketches graced each flanking wall and was illuminated softly with modern track lighting. At the end of the hallway, left or right, floor-to-ceiling French doors pushed open to reveal the oversized bedrooms. I slept in the bedroom to the left. Both were of equal size, and both had an adjoining bathroom. The master bedroom overlooked a courtyard below, and that's the room I slept in. A couple of my neighbors—I really couldn't say which ones—owned that courtyard space and kept a quiet, simple garden of herbs, fruit, and cutting flowers each spring and summer.

I bought my apartment with my first significant bonus many years ago, and what a year that was. That was the year I broke away from the pack and established myself at the top of the advertising agency I worked for and, frankly, at the top of the industry I worked in. I was instrumental to winning a new account with my strategy, my idea, and my campaign. That new account turned into significant fees that year and today represents tens of millions of dollars of income to the agency, nearly 8 percent of our total revenue, in fact. It was my crown jewel. And by it, I mean the apartment. It was my home. It was my sanctuary where I could lock out the world. Most importantly, it was a symbol—*the* symbol—of my success.

It took me exactly fifty-five minutes to get ready for work in the morning, give or take a minute or two. It was always the same: grab my first cup of coffee, plop down in front of my computer to check for new e-mails and any new news that might have broken overnight. That was followed by a small breakfast consisting of oatmeal and a banana along with another cup of coffee. A quick shave, a quicker shower, and pulling on clothes that I had laid out carefully the night before filled my last remaining moments. Then I sat quietly on the chocolate leather couch, preparing myself for the struggle that would be my day. I never really thought consciously about it, but each day was a struggle because I allowed it to be.

My feet hit the Manhattan concrete at around 6:15 AM every morning. This morning was crisp, and the cool air made me cough a little as I took in the outdoor environment with my first great breath of the day. It was my favorite time of year. I enjoyed the first few weeks during any change of season, but the rebirth of spring was by far my favorite. Come to think about it, I had always cherished change, so it was ironic that I eliminated it from my day-to-day life.

There was usually not a soul to be found on my quiet street. I mean, I lived in a city with millions of other people, but I started most days isolated from any of them. Sure, I could see some casual traffic on Central Park West up ahead, but there was very little activity at this hour. I had convinced myself that I left for work so early because of an insatiable dedication to my work, but it was undoubtedly to face as few actual people on the streets as possible.

My route was deliberate and specific. It was deliberately specific. A quick eleven blocks down from 70th Street via Central Park West, and I would always cross town at 59th Street. And I always picked the south side of 59th street because the luxury hotels wouldn't tolerate the homeless vagrants lounging in their breezeways along Central Park South. The Ritz, Helmsley, The Intercontinental, The Plaza—they all had zero-tolerance policies against anyone contaminating the experience of a guest, and that made me comfortably relaxed as I strolled toward the conscious comatose of my work day. I also enjoyed keeping my eye on the prize, fantasizing about arriving in style to spend time in the world's most exclusive club of celebrities, politicians, and captains of trade. To me, money was a natural resource that could be indefinitely replenished through the expense of others, and I was sure it was only a matter of time before I had perfected the process of manufacturing this resource to my satisfaction, whatever the expense.

Once past the park, I occasionally came upon at least one human being sleeping in its own filth, at which point I would cross the street or veer wide away on the sidewalk to avoid being infected with whatever social disease brought someone to this particular point in their life. But I was better than most. At least I noticed them at all.

With a turn right, south down Madison Avenue, a broad cloak of confidence emerged around me, a façade created by money and power. With each short block, I completed the transformation from a frightened, self-loathing frog into a titan of innovation and creativity. My kingdom was at hand, and it started with the doorman who greeted me with admiration and adoration mixed with a hint of awe. Each and every morning I graced his path, and each and every morning he celebrated the "master-and-slave" relationship I had come to expect. The guards inside were not as forthcoming, but I saw them tremble with expectation as I passed through the badge access portico. They knew who I was. Everyone here knew who I was.

As I stepped out of the elevator and out into the broad, bright, and open space of the executive floor, the exuberant rush of control filled me. The average person would pause and even possibly gasp at this breathtaking scene of opulence. I was used to it.

My dense John Lobb soles slapped the hardwoods beneath me, echoing loudly with the pace of my brisk gate toward Nirvana. Most of the administrators that were already at work didn't even dare look in my direction. If they did, it wouldn't matter, as I rarely acknowledged their presence to begin with, even going so far as to outright ignore the occasional "Good morning, sir" as I strolled lavishly toward my office at the very end of the hallway.

I should have had exponentially more empathy for my own personal assistant than I actually did. I just expected her to be there before me, and with me, and for me, always. She greeted me each morning with a broad and sincere smile.

"Good morning, sir. Looking like a top notch day," she would say with just a hint of a forgotten British accent, dramatically muted by years of living in the doldrums of New York City. She always set out a plated offering—coffee, bagel, muffin, fruit. And every day I ignored most of it, and usually all of it.

Settling into my plush leather chair, surrounded by the ramparts of my impressive office—it was impressive, not majestic, but I was on the way to majestic—I always flipped around to stare out of the wall of windows behind me. I sat forty-two floors above the Manhattan streets, looking into the face of another building southeast of my view, but over the tops of most of the other avenues as I looked northeast.

The first thing I always did was check my calendar, which I never quite understood because I never left work without knowing exactly what was scheduled the following day, and I would confirm any changes to the plan by checking my Blackberry several times throughout the evening.

I already knew what was first. It was Monday morning and that meant the 8:00 AM executive staff meeting was only an hour away. I blew out a sigh of annoyance laced with a hint of disdain. I would sit around for an hour and a half and listen to a bunch of "never-weres" prattle on about the state of the agency, even though not one of them was in touch with our people, our clients, and the work we did on their behalf. What was worse, they were clueless about creating ideas that sold soft drinks, fast food, designer clothes, flat screen TVs, or luxury automobiles. They didn't have a clue. But I did. I developed ideas that created the very spirit of consumerism, ideas that fueled the very concept of capitalism.

I was the very heart of this firm, and everyone knew it, but oddly only a few of my executive peers ever acknowledged it openly. It was with this poise and character that I entered the hallowed board room. I always arrived early to coax and coddle the "inner circle" over a cup of coffee or cappuccino. I was not fully or formally a part of the inner circle yet, but I acted the part in every way. It was 8:15 AM before the entire brood of over-bloated blowhards settled into their posh, yet purposeful, positions at the table, each enjoying an unspoken respect for their own wealth and greed. And while I had a seat at the table, it was a very large table, and I was inevitably banished to the far end of the room. But I took comfort in knowing that my face could be seen and my voice could be heard by every single person that mattered to me [sigh].

The executive staff meeting started slowly. It lagged in the middle and expectedly had an anti-climatic finish, much like it did every month. I had such disdain for my executive peers, but it was necessary to pamper and adore them into promoting my agenda. Mostly, I detested who they had become. Lazy, not stupid, but disconnected, which made them incompetent. But I revered what they had—money, power, control. Ironically, I failed to realize the correlation.

They were useful in different ways. I was at a certain time and place in my rise to power where I needed their support, their connections, and most of all, their money. So I sat quietly except to overtly support or validate one bland sentiment after another but never one *over* another. I smiled and nodded in equal and adoring affirmation as they each guffawed about this differentiator and that unique selling proposition. Dinosaurs.

They didn't have the first sense of how to manipulate people in today's fragmented, infinitely niche cultural onslaught, where individuals moved quickly and without warning into and out of different roles in order to satisfy the empty demands their daily lives placed upon them. I studied the faces around the table. No. They didn't understand how to create the need, to design specific choices to be made over infinite choices, or even that it could be designed or, dare I say, created. No. My elitist brethren didn't have a clue. But I did. I knew how to *create* people—or at least characters—that people wanted to be. I knew how to manufacture styles, attitudes, culture itself, down to the underlying needs and wants of the individuals it comprised. I had the uncanny ability to construct the very psyche of a consumer in order to get those consumers to reach deep into their wallets and hand over their hard-earned cash because they wanted to be a part of something … something that others were, or something that others had.

It was hard for me to concentrate on the tiresome discussion going on around me. My thoughts wandered constantly to my next meeting. It was a two-hour brainstorming session I had scheduled as a continuation of one of the most important threads in my life. And that anticipation, coupled with my current state of contempt, created minutes that felt like hours, meaningless blather that felt like cruel and unusual punishment. There we sat, hotly contesting an unwanted overture from a very large global agency network to buy our … very large global agency network. Great. A placebo of productivity—squared. Of course, the outcome had no real implication to the future of this agency and our livelihoods, or at least mine. But it gave these men a sense of purpose, something to be passionate about, even if they had no idea what to do or where to go from here. We were building to a crescendo, but no one knew how the song ended. And then there it was, the summary statement that validated my deepest thoughts. From the lips of our President came the inevitable impotent demand to his executive team. He voiced it with a veiled sense of self-importance and significance, but in reality, it defined the egregious nature of corporate executives trying to operate in a world they did not fully understand because someone else took care of everything.

"Someone send me a three sentence e-mail that I can send to someone!"

As usual, I was that someone that needed to figure out what to write and who to send it to. I always did, and it was always the right thing to say to the right person or people. It just annoyed me to no end that the messenger was always someone else. But at least it brought the executive staff meeting to an end.

I left the boardroom and went straight to my personal conference room to make final preparations for my next meeting. I was leading a large business development team that would be pitching one of the largest retailers in the United States. This was a chance to win a new account that would send me into the stratosphere and forever carve out my position in this firm and solidify a place for me atop this industry. With this win, I was on a certain path to the corner office, but more importantly, my own agency. I didn't just want my name on the door of the corner office; I wanted it on the front door. I wanted it on buildings across the country and around the world. This win would certainly launch me like a ballistic missile toward that dream, and I didn't much think about, or frankly care about, any collateral damage that occurred as a result.

There were already a half dozen people in the large conference room when I arrived. My presence, upon entering the room, fundamentally changed the mood of the group. I loved that. My people paused to acknowledge my arrival, then returned to meticulously preparing the presentation of thoughts and ideas that had been meticulously prepared for weeks upon weeks. The prospect was one of those big "do-it-yourself" home improvement retailers. They were a relative newcomer to the market but quickly rose to the third largest in the country by selling on price and value. But growth had stagnated, and the discount message wasn't effective for a new class of customers.

There were two other well-known brands entrenched ahead of this rising star, but both were collapsing under the weight of their own intemperance and hedonism. And while sleepwalking through a suburban existence, the typical suburbanite knew that he or she wanted to feel as if he or she were part of a small-town community, but that suburbanite also wanted to be treated with respect and esteem for achieving its above-average position in life. This experience was expected everywhere they mindlessly spent their hard-earned money, and particularly in a place where they came to improve upon their most prized possession. That was my angle.

To effectively capture the hearts—and wallets—of the sleepwalking elite, I needed to manufacture a façade of monumental proportions. The average "above-average" consumer was eager to invest heavily in quality products that shaped the very nature of whom they wanted everyone around them to believe they were—happy, wealthy, classy, warm, and friendly. We would design everything around a customer that only wanted the best—or at least things that looked like the best but cost much less—for themselves, their homes, their friends, and their families.

This battle would be fought and won in a different way. I understood that the very above-average lives and memories of the sleepwalkers were unfolding in their kitchens, backyards, and front porches. We would inject a small-town, service-oriented sensibility into the very philosophy, operations, products, and overall image of this monolithic chain. We would construct a carefully choreographed charade that held the customer in the highest admiration—a place that believed your town, your home, your family, your project, and you, personally, were more important than any revenue, profit, or shareholder value. From the advertising campaign to the customer service, from packaging and presentation of products down to details such as the temperature of the stores, how and where customers stood in line to purchase merchandise, the uniforms, hairstyles, and even accents of the associates on the floor, I would create an experience that cared about you personally with the volume and efficiency of a big box retailer. That's what it would take for the sleepwalkers to be thankful for our great manipulation.

And I had no doubt about the effectiveness of this approach. I incessantly studied specific aspects of human behavior and even required my people to personally visit, shop, and just generally hang around for hundreds of hours in hundreds of suburban stores across the country, diligently cataloging the slightest needs, common behaviors, and expectations of the average above-average consumer. Every now and again, I would join them on these perverse ethnographic safaris.

It was brilliant, and I was at the helm. I was brilliant. It would make them richer. More importantly, it would make me richer. And I knew wealth was the critical ingredient to power ... which was a prerequisite for absolute control. I was the leader, but the agency had assembled a very large team of the brightest, most strategic and creative thinkers we had. I valued only a handful of perspectives in the room; the rest were baggage, but you've got to take bags on every trip, otherwise how would your stuff get from one place to another?

With only two weeks remaining before the core team flew out to make our pitch, we were finished. We were ready. And we would spend the next two weeks making our very best thoughts and ideas even better. Of course, there would be distractions. Existing clients, employee reviews, executive staff meetings. But I would spend every free minute from now until then improving my pitch. There was nothing more important to me than this: this pitch, this win, this new client. This would create a windfall of cash and recognition, and I would need to invest both in creating the "future me" I so badly desired.

Chapter 2

Anna woke up feeling different. Then again, Anna woke up every morning feeling different, so today was no different. She groaned quietly as she pulled herself from beneath her fluffy down comforter and dragged her feet eleven steps to the small bathroom, which happened to be the only room with a door in the 650-square-foot studio apartment. The apartment was located on the top floor of a beautiful Victorian Italianate. Anna had rented this little corner of the world from Ms. Sue for the past few years. She appreciated the quaint little apartment and adored the grand, old home. But most of all, Anna loved living in the heart of Pacific Heights.

Looking into the mirror, Anna took in a deep breath and let out a long, strong sigh, blowing her bangs upward with the last bit of breath out of her thin, dry lips. As she brushed her teeth, she thought briefly about her disheveled hair, which then led to thoughts about her disheveled life. She was turning thirty this week. She had no husband, much less a boyfriend. No house, much less a real apartment. She had held twelve different jobs since graduating from Berkeley eight years ago. Too proud to take *too much* charity from her wealthy parents, Anna consigned herself to working for one beleaguered not-for-profit after the next. Glancing at the clock, she knew she would be late for work at her current one … again.

Anna paused briefly at the top of the dimly lit, narrow staircase to consider how she had arrived at this particular place in her life. Unwilling to let these thoughts ruin her day, Anna quickly shrugged them off and bounded down the tiny steps that led to the small garage below.

Due to her advanced age, Ms. Sue no longer carried the burden of car ownership and was kind enough to let Anna park her little black Jetta in the garage. But the garage held decades of furniture and belongings from Ms. Sue's past lives, so Anna's old Jetta was a snug fit. So tight, in fact, she often had to enter and exit through the window because there was just not enough room to open the car door. But Anna didn't care. It was extraordinarily convenient, and she was happy to have a safe place to put her car at night.

As she backed out onto the narrow part of Clay Street, Anna had fleeting thoughts of skipping work again. She would much rather watch the tourists bump and bumble along Fisherman's Wharf in search of great food and some entertainment. To her, *they* were the entertainment. Or maybe she would quietly take in views of the city from atop Alta Plaza; after all, the park was only a short walk from her home.

But her annoying sense of responsibility kept Anna driving ahead, and by the time she hit the Embarcadero, she was once again second-guessing most of the choices in her life, which became more like obsessive thoughts as she crossed the Bay Bridge toward her not-for-profit work in Berkeley. As I-80 turned north, traffic slowed to a crawl, then periodically stopped altogether. With each mile that crept slowly by, Anna felt an overwhelming urge to exit her current life and speed due east toward an unknown destination, an unknown future. Her frustrations with the traffic, her job, and her life threatened to overwhelm her.

Then something up ahead pulled her away from those distracting thoughts. It was a car on the shoulder. The hood was open on an old, white Oldsmobile. It was hard to see what the problem was, but there was a tower of white smoke billowing from the engine. As she came closer, she saw an older man in a ratty, old suit. He looked detached and dejected as he stared at the dead or dying engine.

This was just the excuse Anna had been looking for all morning. She put on her blinker and softly tossed her bangs aside as she carefully looked over her right shoulder and glided onto the shoulder.

Anna was apprehensive. She pulled up slowly behind the broken-down car but stayed far enough behind in case it happened to burst into flames. She got out and cautiously approached the man, studying him intently as she approached, but he did not even acknowledge her presence with a glance. He looked harmless enough, even a bit pitiable. He was a person in need, and Anna had yet to shy away from anyone who needed a helping hand.

"That looks bad," Anna declared, waving the smoke away from her face.

"It's not as bad as you might think," he answered.

She raised her eyes, not knowing the first thing about how bad it was or wasn't.

"Can I call someone for you?" she persisted. "A tow truck, maybe?"

"No thanks. I don't have that kind of money," he said, remaining intently focused on the smoldering engine. "There's a garage just south of here. I'm just gonna walk down to the next exit and pick up a hose and some coolant. That should do it."

Anna thought about this briefly and then blurted out, "Well, hop in then. I'll take you."

For the first time since their encounter, the man took his eyes off the steaming engine and connected with the petite young woman. They stared at one another for just a few seconds before he smiled and said, "Well now, that would be right helpful."

Anna waved him toward her car. He glanced briefly at it and only started moving when she said, "Let's get going."

As Anna pulled back onto the freeway, the concern she had about letting this complete stranger into her car eased slightly when he immediately recognized the music playing softly in the background.

"Is this Sydney Bechet?" the old man asked, pointing at the CD player.

"Why, yes, it is," she replied a bit surprised. "Are you a fan?"

"I am a fan of anything that brings joy into the world, and Mr. Bechet has brought a lot of joy into the world."

Anna smiled and felt that joy as she listened to the French jazz musician and watched the white Oldsmobile fade in the rearview mirror. Free from the monotony of her workday once again, Anna now went unbothered into the dense morning traffic as she navigated the Jetta back south toward San Francisco.

"My name is Anna," she continued.

"That's a right fine name, Anna," he replied, nodding. "And I am Noah."

"Sorry about your car."

"That's okay," he said. "Good things happened today."

Anna didn't understand his comment at first, so she chose to let it float in her mind for a few minutes before responding. She was always thoughtful that way, never reactive, and keenly interested in the true meaning behind the words others spoke to her. Her pondering was interrupted.

"So, why do you do what you do, Anna?" Noah asked with genuine interest. His carefree smile and disposition had turned more serious.

This was not a cliché, small-talk question. It was more like he knew exactly what she did and why she did it, and it caught Anna off guard. Her anxiety unexpectedly spiked as she thought about her work, her idiosyncratic lifestyle, and her decision to pick up this stranger in need. Noah's question was incredibly direct and a bit strange. It definitely demanded some clarification.

"What, exactly, do you mean?"

"Your work, Anna. Why do you do it?"

"How do you know what I do?" Now she was getting a little nervous, and she instinctively slowed the car down.

"I don't." His intense expression changed to a bright, knowing smile. "Just thought I would ask about your work. And I'm not really interested in what you do, but why you do it."

Anna relaxed again, then regretted feeling threatened by this gentle old man. She tossed a quick smile his way, a nonverbal apology he readily accepted.

"I work for a small nonprofit organization. We help other nonprofits in the area raise money and show them how to get the most out of limited resources." She paused, hoping that would satisfy the question, but the puzzled look on Noah's face prompted her to explain further.

"I've always worked for nonprofits. In fact, I've worked at a bunch of them ... saving whales, forests, the poor, the homeless, the sick. But each of them always felt less like a sincere cause and more like a mechanism for a few wealthy, educated individuals to feel a little less guilty about their wealth and education. And I hated choosing one cause over another, so I was happy to find work that can make a positive, meaningful difference for so many different causes."

There was a long pause as Anna didn't know what else to say.

Then Noah spoke to clarify his position. "Surely there are many causes worthwhile. Like this thing I read about recently, some guy from MIT has promised a laptop for every child. Now that's a cause rooted in selflessness ... and resourcefulness. I mean, putting the world's knowledge at the fingertips of poverty-stricken children across the world can definitely change the world." Noah paused and patted a little tune on the dashboard with his fingers. "After all, passion often leads to action, and the purpose for helping is often more important than the cause itself. So that brings me back to the question you still haven't answered young lady. *Why* do you do what you do?"

Anna thought quietly about this for a moment. She let her thoughts meander carelessly in her head, and then she let them race with intensity and precision. She knew exactly why she did what she did; she just didn't want to tell *him*.

Anna grew up in Southern gentry. Her parents were wealthy, conservative Southerners, born and raised in Louisiana. They were deeply religious and endlessly capitalistic and had settled in New Orleans to build their life together. Anna was born into providence from her parents' perspective, and expectations for her were very high. But she was a debutante who never quite realized her full potential, whatever that was and whatever that meant, to anyone other than herself.

The comparison was tough, however. Her father was a well-liked and brilliant businessman who successfully invested in a broad range of industries that included agriculture, construction, and even retail. Their income afforded her mother the opportunity to apply her initiative, drive, and striking beauty to leading nearly every major social and charitable event across the state. This wasn't real charity work, just elitist parties that allowed the Louisiana privileged to display their unmatched kindness and generosity.

Anna hated the comparison. She resented her father's destructive obsession with money and the power it afforded him. She loathed how their wealth distorted her mother's beauty and grace. Anna saw the world differently, and she never hesitated to bring that to the attention of anyone that would listen, particularly her own mother and father. And when the fighting had become too much, Anna was sent to spend the summer with her mother's "free spirit" sister, Emma, in the great city of San Francisco when Anna was just sixteen years old.

For over five years, Anna lived with her wealthy, eccentric aunt. Anna spent her days at school, and her nights and weekends were dedicated to helping support Aunt Emma's freelance social work. There was always a needy soul gracing the front porch in search of a job, an education, or just a bite to eat. But as the cancer took hold, Aunt Emma retreated from the exhausting demands of helping others. Ultimately, she was even unable to spend any quality time with her best friend, Ms. Sue, opting instead to apply what remaining strength she had to creating her art and poetry.

The only regret Anna had in her life so far was that the cancer took her kindred spirit away less than six months before she graduated from Berkeley. And when Aunt Emma died, so did any real connection that Anna had with her parents.

Noah sensed the dissonance in the silence. "Sometimes you need to meet on the very bridge you burned in order to reconcile your differences. And my mama always used to say, 'Destroying a bridge is easy. Any damn fool can do it with a bucket of gas and a book of matches. But building a bridge takes skill, resourcefulness, collaboration, and perseverance.'"

"She sounds like a smart woman."

"She is, Anna. She is."

Anna smiled as she thought about the simple wisdom of an older generation, or maybe it was the complex insight of an extraordinary person. After all, there were extraordinary people in the world; she was certain about that. Anna caught glimpses of these kinds of profound thoughts occasionally and would expound upon them to herself when she had the time, but they never amounted to much. *We can all be extraordinary if we just try a little bit.* And then the fleeting insight was gone.

"Come to think of it," Noah continued, "I would be most thankful if you wouldn't mind dropping me at her house. It's not *too* far."

Anna didn't hesitate. "That would be fine."

This would certainly keep Anna from making it to work at all today, but she was not worried about getting to a job she really cared nothing about. And besides, something drew her to Noah, which was not unusual. Anna was often drawn to random people and experiences and ironically chased these aimless directions in hopes of finding a more meaningful and permanent purpose for her own life. She was deeply intrigued by Noah's company and was quite certain that Noah and his wise, old mother held the answers she was seeking.

"Where does she live?"

Noah pushed back into his seat, pulled his old hat down over his face, and closed his eyes. "Louisiana."

Chapter 3

Crazy. That's what I thought I was growing up, in the confines of suburban normalcy. The affluent neighborhoods of suburban Chicago were breeding grounds for the structured, the planned, and the thoughtless over-scheduling. I suppose that's why I resisted the very concept of structure from an early age. But unconsciously, the order was being cast as an inescapable frame in my own mind. I had always had a surging curiosity about all of life's complexities, the curiosity coursing from one synaptic gap to the next in an endless introspection. But my own analytical tendencies, undoubtedly nurtured by my social context, inevitably drowned my desire for spontaneity and adventure. Caution controlled my life, creating repetition and routine like a well-tuned machine. And that was the glorifying yet horrifying paradox I faced as a young boy.

I remember vividly when I was young—maybe eight or nine—my father asked me to help hang some heavy curtains in his bedroom. I was thrilled, honored to help my Dad, even though I understood the dangers such an assignment might bring. After all, he was as short on handyman skills as he was on patience.

As expected, he struggled mightily with the measuring, the leveling, and the drilling, growing more and more frustrated and impatient as the progress slowed. Then, all of his efforts and my looking on in anticipation came to an abrupt end when the bulky power drill refused to fit behind the curtain rod support.

"Get me a Phillips-head screwdriver," he commanded, looking down from atop the step ladder. Calmness surrounded his directive. Excitement overcame me as the importance of such a task rooted itself in my attention.

"Quickly!" he barked as I sat frozen with wonder, thinking about the important task I had just been given. "It's the one that has the little star at the end, and *not* the flat one."

I flew from the bedroom and scampered through the hall, then down the stairs. But my focus was soon derailed, as it often was, as I passed the kitchen on the way to the garage. My mother stopped me with her immobilizing voice.

"Hey there ... where are you going so fast? Why don't you rest for a second and have something refreshing with me."

"Like what?" I was always in the mood for whatever my mother was serving, and her attention obscured anything else I might be doing at any given point in time.

"I don't know, a little milk, some juice ..." and then she paused with an adoringly wicked little grin, "or maybe a homemade milkshake?"

The shake sounded great, but as the first scoop of ice cream hit the bottom of the blender, my mother and I simultaneously jerked our eyes toward the thunderous roar above us, followed by an unnatural screeching, then a loud slam. My father immediately went to "launch codes," showering verbal abuse down on almost everything in his path.

Immediately, I remembered the screwdriver as I looked helplessly at my mother, who was incapable of helping me, as she innocently smiled while continuing to blend the cold whole milk and ice cream. It was too late. He was already down the stairs and coming right for me. I shook slightly in fear as he grabbed my arm abruptly, hard enough that it kind of hurt, but it scared me even more. He bent down and looked me straight in the eyes; beads of sweat had gathered on his intensely-pierced forehead.

"Life is full of pain, boy, and you must make a choice. You can enjoy the pain of discipline and reap its many benefits, or you can drag around the pain of regret and never achieve what you were meant to be."

It's amazing how such things can be imprinted on you, casting a profound and lasting effect on the trajectory of your life. That lesson was never mentioned again—no further explanation, no clarification, not even an accompanying caveat. But I worked to practice these words in the best way I knew how, without ever really understanding what they meant. In many ways, I built my life around those words, and they often took me in the most perverse directions.

Throughout my life, I acknowledged and even carefully nurtured *it* to *its* fullest. But I could never surface it enough for me to recognize it fully. And even if it did, I doubt I had the tools to understand it anyway. It grew like a fertile weed, the pressure building, refusing to be ignored, like a small sprout bursting from its seed, or the contents of a champagne bottle shaken repeatedly. It pushed from the inside out, and the pressure was mounting within the walls of my mind, all the way through college, into graduate school, and even during my rise to power in New York. Today, I was tormented by my success in this foreign land, and I blamed my parents for every bit of it … because I was told to. Ridiculous. Routine ruled my life. Routine was the bondage I unwittingly allowed to tie me down. Control freed me from my real thoughts about life, about living. Hunting helped me escape both.

For those reasons, among a lifetime of others, I awoke that fateful Tuesday morning in March as I did for the past 5,211 days before at 5:14 AM sharp with the smell of cappuccino floating into the bedroom of my upper west side apartment. Don't ask me why I set my alarm clock at exactly fourteen minutes past five because I don't know. Most likely so I did not experience a bit of deviation from the sequence. Outside, there were familiar noises—an occasional dog barked, a faint car alarm sounded, intermittent honking. The City was just starting to stir, and I was once again getting ready to join its choreographed monotony for reasons I never resisted, even though they asphyxiated my proper place in the world.

As I lay in my bed, smothered in the security of my own home, something deafening happened inside. The loudest and most obtrusive silence dragged me from my deep sleep and launched me immediately into the conscious living. I jerked my covers up close and hid further into my bed, clutching my hands together in an attempt to relieve this intense sense of disorder.

My eyes darted around the room, nervously looking for the deviation. Nothing was out of place, but I knew something was different. I closed my eyes tightly and bit my bottom lip as I struggled to regain control over the moment, hoping to make it all go away. But something was happening, something I had not experienced in many, many years. It plunged into the room, into my body, and into my soul. Something was *different* today.

It was unusual, and I didn't notice the urge at first, but it grew with strength as the seconds of this particular morning ticked forward, each second leaving the next behind. Something amazing was happening: an urge. Actually, it was more like an extraordinary event, a supernatural call to change the routine. I felt a powerful insistence to stop the sequence. Lying there alone, I slowly accepted the fact that this feeling would not be denied.

My mind shot right to the implications. I had not missed a day of work since I set my feet into New York City over fourteen years ago.

Work was my haven. I excelled at work like no other part of my life. I *wanted* to go to work. I *needed* to go to work. But the need to break the routine on this morning was simply too great.

Enough. I got out of bed and headed to the kitchen, scooping up my iPhone from the mantle along the way. Sitting at the kitchen table, I stared blankly at my contacts list, not believing what I was about to do. There was only one ring and then an immediate answer. A familiar soft voice on the other end was ready at my beckon.

"Good morning, sir. Everything alright?"

"Everything is fine," I paused, tracing an arbitrary outline on the table with my finger. "But, please reschedule my meetings and hold all of my calls. I … I won't be in today."

No response. Only silence for what seemed an eternity. I wasn't compelled to fill the quiet space with any words of my own, so I waited, continuing to trace that arbitrary figure on my kitchen table, which had now started to establish itself more permanently as the oils from my finger permeated the wood grain.

"Sir?" was the singular reply. A simple word said in a way that begged clarification to an absurdly confusing situation. Ordinarily, an ordinary person calling in to miss a day of an ordinary job was, well, ordinary. But this was an extraordinary event, and I knew it would set off a chain reaction of extraordinary size throughout the firm.

Finally, more words from her. "Are you not feeling well?"

"I feel fine. I just need the day off to attend to some personal matters. Nothing serious, just a few personal items I need to deal with today."

I found that using the word *personal* was usually enough to keep even the nosiest individual from inquiring further about my personal business. And this instance was no different.

"But what about the pitch? You have two separate working sessions scheduled today and the team has been up half the night preparing your revisions from yesterday."

"It will have to wait. Let everyone take it easy today, and we'll assemble first thing tomorrow morning. The work is in great shape, and there is still over a week left before we go live, so no worries. Be sure everyone is fresh and ready to go in the morning. Better have everyone block the entire morning. We'll want to do a deep dive on everything, start to finish."

More silence.

"Yes, sir. I will let everyone know."

"Uh ..."

"Yes, sir?"

"Not everyone." I was certain she understood this direct order. The last thing I needed was the executive team getting nervous, or worse, questioning my commitment altogether.

"No, sir. Not everyone. But word travels fast."

"Of course it does. See you tomorrow."

I ended the call without hearing a final response. I ended my thoughts about work just as quickly and turned my attention to the day before me. What was I doing? *Get dressed,* I thought to myself, *then go from there.*

As I pulled on my old, familiar cargo pants and a soft cotton sweater, I thought about a walk in the park. The idea came to me immediately. Actually, it's more like I was brought to the idea, and the idea was comforting. A walk in the park was exactly what I was going to do. With excitement and anticipation, I gathered my things and threw on a sweatshirt and cross trainers before heading out.

My optimism of things to come was building as I burst into the cool March air, but as I stepped off the last stair of my stoop, my security evaporated. My senses intensified, as they always did, and I was ready for battle. Less than a block from Central Park, I knew the walk would do me good, maybe even clear my head a little. Sure, it was Tuesday morning, and I *only* walked in the park on Saturday afternoon because the street urchins seemed to overrun the tranquil sense of stability most every other day, especially during the week, and *particularly on Tuesdays.*

As my left foot left the final stair and hit the concrete in front of me, all of my energy was focused on scanning my immediate surroundings for any sign of trouble, regardless of its size. My discerning eye noticed every tick and flicker, preparing me for the slightest threat or disruption of the balance. All clear.

I moved easily to Central Park West without encountering a single human being. And before I had even noticed, my legs carried me past the small stone entrance of "The Park" at 72nd Street. The narrow, asphalt path was damp from the morning dew as I circled past Strawberry Fields. An occasional bird chirped, settled somewhere in the wiry throngs of the bare tree branches overhead. Some were budding, but mostly the foliage and trees were still reeling from the harsh New York winter.

I was not headed in any particular direction but simply followed the path in front of me. And before too long, I was strolling alongside

The Lake. Heading toward the Boathouse was the plan for now. I would enjoy a cup of coffee and take in whatever ducks were strong enough to brave the winter; there were always a few that did.

The Boathouse was only sparsely populated at this hour in the morning. There were a few tourists having an over-priced breakfast, and the wait staff busied themselves preparing for the day's rush. No matter; my coffee was warm and sweet as it circulated in my mouth, and it warmed my chest as I swallowed.

The Park was peaceful. I reflected now, as I often did, about the tranquility of this place nestled in the chaotic surrounding of New York City. It was the ultimate juxtaposition of man and nature cohabitating rather peacefully together in this unforgiving space. Prior to 1857, The Park lay dormant, waiting patiently to be born from nothing more than a rock-filled swamp that lay isolated miles north of the bustling city that was largely packed in below 38th Street. The need for such a space, a quiet retreat from the cramped and chaotic daily grind, emerged out of the mouths of men such as William Cullen Bryant and Andrew Jackson Downing, and while the actual design of The Park came from the brilliant minds of men like Frederick Law Olmstead and Calvert Vaux, the real magic flowed from the hearts and hands of thousands that would carve out, enhance, and maintain its beauty over decades.

Lost in my own thoughts, I did not notice the time or space that had brought me to the southern edge of a densely wooded area known as The Ramble. To be frank, there were not many steps of the park I had not walked before. In fact, each Saturday, I roamed its perfectly ordered design in an attempt to scrub the dissonance from my mind that had accumulated over the week. This usually amounted to no more than cataloging the steps I took, mapping a little more familiar terrain each time out while avoiding the benign threats around me. To this point, however, I had always avoided The Ramble.

Today, my mind was incredibly preoccupied with the change in sequence, the disorder, and, ironically, my desire to control the unknown with a familiar routine led me into an area that was not at all familiar. But the inherent beauty and tranquility around me shrouded a deepening need to panic. Then, a bright yellow bird flickered just yards away in the wires of a barren hedge. As an amateur birdwatcher—and birdwatching really was nothing more than another way to catalog life around me—I recognized this little guy to be a Western Oriole, which was quite rare for this area. Trying to get a better look at this noteworthy bird, I stepped off the path momentarily, craning my neck in order to get a better view, but it was gone.

As I turned back to continue my journey, the path before me was gone. It had vanished, and I was standing alone in the woods; dense trees and brush obscured my sight in every direction. And in an instant, the panic within me flowed, overloading my senses and short circuiting my ability to think rationally.

Amidst one of the most arresting parks in the country and arguably one of the most magnificent settings in the world, I began to panic. Paralyzed, I momentarily tried to rationalize that only a few steps, an acre at most, separated me from one of the most densely populated cities in the world. My heart was racing, which in turn caused my mind to race, which in turn triggered my instinctual "fight or flight" response.

My sense of direction obscured, I unknowingly pushed deeper into the thicket. The cold, breezy air chilled the sweat that had formed around my head and neck as I began running, slowly at first, more frenetically now, as the leaves and dry winter limbs cracked beneath my feet.

I began hyperventilating, taking in short, rapid breaths as my chaotic attempt to escape the situation only thrust me deeper into the unknown. My hands were throbbing as I frantically pushed the branches and vines from my face, as if I were attempting to violently rip the self-loathing from my soul. For God's sake, I was lost in the woods in the middle of New York City.

Frantic now, I was running flat out with my head down and my hands outstretched, shielding my face. My eyes were partially closed, but I could sense that the clearing was getting closer as the dry branches scratched at my skin with an unmerciful tenacity. I had to make the clearing. That's all I could think about. With a final surge, I burst through the thick brush and fell to my knees, the sweat stinging the scratches on my hands and face.

After only an instant there on my knees, I looked up, and there he was, sitting on top of an overturned milk carton under an old blue tarp, roasting what looked to be a sausage over a small fire burning inside an oversized coffee can. He was poking at his meal with a small stick clutched in his dirty, worn hands. Intense fear and anxiety rushed into me with each quick breath that seared my lungs. There I was, an uninvited guest that had just crashed into the house of a man with no home. And there he was, an uninvited guest that had just crashed into the life of a man that was not really alive.

We sat staring awkwardly at each other for what seemed like an eternity. His face was covered with a large and illustrious salt and pepper beard, accented with dirt, grass, and the prior night's meal. An old, worn wool coat covered his hulking body down to his black boots, coveralls underneath. Standing up and looming ominously over me, he took in a large breath and unexpectedly blew out a single word.

"Welcome."

His dirty hands were now extended toward me. Without thinking, as if I were being forced to surrender my own inhibitions, my hands moved slowly toward his. Resistance was futile. The tips of my fingers made their way toward his, then the fingers themselves, and finally my palms found a comfortable place in his. Time slowed, then stopped altogether, as our flesh met, our hands pressed together, our eyes locked. My soul was emerging; his was already everlasting.

"I am glad you are here," came the next words at last. "I have been waiting for you for a very long time."

I could not respond. I was frozen. I did not understand.

"My name is Noah."

Coming to my senses, I jerked my hands from his. I sprang to my feet and my eyes darted around the small clearing looking for any means of escape. Not immediately seeing an exit, I bought some time and distance with a few words.

"I'm ... I'm very sorry for ... having disrupted you," I said as I began to circle around this man toward a small path I could now see behind him. "I was ... I got a little turned around, you see ..."

"It's no problem," he quickly interrupted, softly backing away from me, sensing my need for retreat. "Really."

I continued slowly toward the path that was now only a few feet away. I even thought about simply running away, down that path and back to a life I left behind only a couple of hours ago. But I hesitated. For some reason, against every impulse in my mind and body, I stopped.

"You don't have to go," he continued. He grabbed a small wooden box and shoved it in my direction. "Would you mind staying for just awhile and giving an old man some much needed company?"

I stood staring a Noah for a second, then ultimately abandoned my fear and gave into his irresistible influence. I reluctantly grabbed the box and sat down cautiously, only a foot or two from his milk carton.

"There now," he continued. "Isn't that better? Aren't we comfortable now?"

I didn't know what to say. Noah went back to his carton, back to his stick and back to poking his sausage that was now charred on one side. He didn't say a word but waited for me to speak. I didn't know what to say.

"So, you are a homeless man then?" I wanted the words back as soon as they left my mouth.

Noah immediately stopped fiddling with the sausage. All of his attention was now focused on me. I was certain he was offended.

"I am a man. And yes, I am homeless. But I am a man nonetheless. And yet I am more than a man because of my orientation. Not my sexual preference, not my political affiliation, nor my monetary position, or any other temporal claim of superiority. My uniqueness exists in my perspective. My *transcendental* orientation."

I was a bit stunned, further regretting my opening question.

"I'm sorry. I'm nervous. And to be perfectly honest, I'm a little scared."

Noah seemed to appreciate my honesty.

"Fear is the poison that kills empathy, compassion, and hospitality," he continued, flipping his sausage without skipping a beat. "We've created a social system where meaningful acts, the things that really matter, are not only underappreciated, but often go completely unnoticed." He turned his attention to me once again. Not a glance, but his full, powerful gaze covered me with deliberation.

"And fear has stolen even that from our hearts … from our actions."

He let the words hang in the air for a minute or two before continuing on.

"Life can be fostered under very simple care instructions: love, kindness, and understanding. But unfortunately, that's not enough anymore. We want everything the other guy has, and we want it right now, whether or not we deserve any of it, or more importantly, whether or not we even actually *need* it."

My anxiety was at an all-time high, but Noah was comforting to me in ways I did not yet understand. As the minutes passed and as his words continued, my fear slowly subsided. My interest grew, and my heart opened. I didn't know what I was doing, but I knew it was good.

"Noah," I paused, searching delicately for the right words, "you have such a fascinating perspective on the world. What are you doing here?"

"I'm cooking this here sausage and getting ready to eat it," he said without hesitation. "Or at least half of it, the other half is for you if you want it."

I couldn't believe that he just offered me half of his meal when it was apparent he had no idea when or where his next meal would come from. But that was not the point. I forged on, this time more bluntly.

"That's not exactly what I meant. What I meant was … how did you get to this place in your life … to this lost, forgotten state?"

Noah stopped. I couldn't tell if he was hurt, offended, or intrigued. He seemed to search his mind for answers, tracing what was sure to have been a long and winding path to this makeshift camp in Central Park. But his words were not what I expected.

"There are many lost and forgotten people in the world, but we are neither lost nor forgotten, just ignored. My guess is I could ask you exactly, and I mean precisely, the same question." Noah paused for a moment to let his point sink in. "I am neither lost nor forgotten," he continued with force, "I know where I am, where I've been, and where I am headed. And it's my love for humanity that carries me from one place to the next." Noah turned back to the sausage. "Dang. Now look at that. Burned. You want half of this or what?"

"No. No, thank you," I said looking at the charred little sausage. "But I am hungry. Come on. Let me buy you a decent meal. I know a place nearby we can shake off the chill and warm our bellies with some good food."

Noah eagerly accepted and was halfway down the little path before I even finished my sentence.

Going forth from the lost and forgotten confines of Noah's homelessness deep within Central Park, we emerged onto Columbus circle amidst the lost and forgotten confines of New York City. The streets were crowded with people hustling to their next appointment, yet we went completely unnoticed within the focused bustle of the city. That is, until we pushed through the doors of the Columbus Circle Deli; then, we were more like rock stars. Well, sort of. No one could take their eyes off of us, but no one wanted to approach us either.

We picked a quiet booth in the back, far away from at least twenty or thirty prying eyes. Noah's presence was sensed throughout the space, but I didn't notice any other person in the diner as I sat directly across from this old man. I was now consumed with Noah's physical attributes.

As Noah studied the laminated menu in front of him, I studied his face, looking for clues about its origin, its journey, and its meaning to me here and now. It was far more severe than I had noticed before, but somehow more comforting now than in the first moments I gazed upon it in the park. I noticed its details, like several half circle wrinkles in each corner of his mouth, which remained slightly obscured by his unkempt beard. His tongue, darker pink than most I've noticed ... not that I remember anyone's tongue specifically, but his seemed richer, more important, and it had plenty to say.

My gazing and reflection were interrupted by a short, stout woman. With the small pad in one hand and a rather large pen in the other, she said quite simply, "What'll you have?"

She busily inscribed Noah's order as he rattled through a half dozen items on the menu. She took my order and, barely looking up, grabbed the menus off the table. "It'll be right up."

Alone once again, the pressure to speak began to mount. I had so many questions, so many curiosities, even a few deep thoughts. But through all of this sorting of information in my mind came my next ridiculous sentence.

"So you live in The Park?"

Noah stopped sorting his silverware, took a sip of his coffee, paused, and reflected on that delicious sip, then looked me right in the eyes.

"Yes. I live in the park, and in the hearts of men." A small smile emerged as the words were pushed from his mouth through the power of that dark, pink tongue.

The waitress interrupted again, a set of plates spanned across her outstretched arm. She dropped them off one by one on the table in front of us, then disappeared as quickly as she had appeared.

Blind to the obvious, I stirred my coffee as my thoughts were redirected to the cool evening that was quickly turning into a cold night as it always did in March. A slight rain started to fall outside, and I searched for words to once again break our uncomfortable silence.

"They just don't do enough about the homeless issue in this country."

Unbelievable. Decades of education, years of professional experience and just plain living in the world, and that's what I had to offer.

"How can you say that?" came the low, somewhat smug reply as Noah looked away from me and down at his portfolio of plates, which were now half empty. His response was not expected.

"You don't agree?" I tried to remain confident in the point I was making, however shallow and immaterial it was.

Noah's eyes darted from his food to connect with my eyes. His sharp gaze penetrated the moment.

"I don't believe homelessness is the issue," he countered. "It is just one passé symptom of a larger wave of social plagues that have been building for centuries. Yet no one recognizes, and therefore addresses, the real problems facing the human condition. You see, I believe there is a fundamental deterioration of the individual that masks our ability to see past superficial concerns like homelessness, joblessness, poverty, crime, racial tension ... the list is long. But it is fear, lack of accountability, entitlement, and a fading sense of spiritual connection that drives a collective need to dissociate, isolate, and hermetically seal our lives off one from another. Those are the true social problems of today, and they reside in each of us. Like many pandemics, our inability to effectively respond to the disease creates the visual symptoms you see lying in our streets, rotting in our prisons or standing forever in our welfare lines."

"I am ... I am ... stunned," I stuttered.

"Besides, aren't you a part of *they?*" Noah wasn't about to stop there. "My sense tells me you are a well-educated and, for the most part, morally sound individual. But you are a slave to routine and control, which manifests itself from fear, which isolates you from others, which, in turn, imprisons your spirit and allows you—actually propels you—to place the problem at *their* feet."

I sat stunned by the accurate portrait Noah had just painted after spending only a few hours in my company. But instead of feeling awed, I was defensive.

"Well, I am here with you," I countered, my eyes squinting, searching for a bit of positive response in his face.

His huge smile returned.

"Yes, you are here with me." He even laughed a big, but short, laugh, which was followed by a heavy pause that hung heavily in the air. "But it is difficult for you, or anyone for that matter, to overcome the centuries of erosion in your faith, the winds of ignoring what we know to be true, battering the bastions of belief minute by minute through our days at school, work, and other public places. Before anyone has been able to recognize the silent thief in the night, it has stolen the very nature of man: that which makes us good, that which makes us true and just. Just as no one wants to acknowledge the secret mistress, it is tolerated, ignored, excused, or explained away. I mean, what are we so afraid of?!"

This last phrase was delivered loudly, accompanied by his fist slamming the table and rattling the plates and silverware. We—and by we I mean Noah—were now gathering stares from the last remaining customers and staff left in the diner.

"Deterioration," he continued in a quieter voice meant for just me. "Deterioration of the individual starts with the abstinence from true faith; that's what destroys us without us even knowing. It's like boiling a frog."

"Boiling a frog?" I didn't follow.

"Sure. You know. If you toss a frog into hot water, he'll struggle to escape. But if you set him in tepid water, he'll sit there calmly as the temperature rises, and he'll never even perceive a difference in the temperature as he's boiled to death."

I shuddered at the thought.

"It's time we lock arms and confront a new wave of social decay, move beyond the so called social ills of the past. 'They don't do enough for the homeless in this country,' what a myopic point of view. We don't do enough about spiritual suicide, isolationism, and self-loathing. Not everyone needs a hit song, popular TV show, Academy Award, or Super Bowl victory. People need each other. We need to do more to love ourselves and each other, to simply be good. It's the selfless act that sparks a fire of faith that burns out of control."

Noah's words were interrupted by a strange chirping. At first I didn't recognize the sound that usually triggered an exact and immediate response from me no matter what situation I happened to be in. There it was again, then again. Unconsciously, I reached into my pocket and answered my phone. Instantly, I was pulled away from this distant place and was right back in my old life.

"Hello?"

"Sir?" came the pretty voice with just a hint of a forgotten British accent.

"Yes. What is it?"

"I just wanted to let you know the team will be ready first thing tomorrow morning. Everyone has accepted; we will have one hundred percent participation, and everyone will be assembled in the main conference room sharply at 8:00 AM."

I paused briefly.

"Great," I finally replied with little enthusiasm, and possibly a hint of disdain. Looking in Noah's direction, I could see he was now clearly annoyed.

"Sir, is … are you okay?"

"Everything is fine. I will see you bright and early tomorrow morning. Good night," and with that, the call was over.

Noah was gathering his simple belongings. "It's late. Time for me to move on," he said, pushing one of the plates away.

The evening had faded, and it was officially a new night.

"Wait," I responded with a hint of desperation. "You can't sleep out there tonight."

We turned to face the window simultaneously, it was raining hard now and only a few degrees separated this hard rain from a hard snow.

"You got a better idea?" He asked, his head back, eyebrows raised and eyes looking down the bridge of his nose at me.

The ultimatum came with force. I knew it was coming, in the same way you know when a punch is coming. You can anticipate the feeling, but it's always more painful and surprising when the knuckles find their mark. Sure, I had a better idea, but I didn't have the nerve to suggest what it was. Or did I?

"You could ..." I started looking at him, somehow trying to measure my tolerance versus actual risk, calibrating each against my fear.

"Yes?" he genuinely looked confused, but earnestly waited for a response.

I wanted to say, "There must be shelters ... ," but instead I blurted out, "You could stay with me."

Noah looked stunned, then slowly stopped gathering his things and eased back into his seat.

"Me? Stay with you?" he asked, looking caught somewhere between disbelief and euphoria. It's like he expected a cruel punch line to an offensive joke while holding out hope for a happy ending.

"Yes. Stay with me tonight," I insisted. "We will take care of tomorrow ... well, tomorrow," I said with a faint smile.

We stared at each other, sharing a mutually magnificent moment, albeit a mutually confusing moment.

"Well, I accept," he said at last, the grand smile broadening once again across his face.

Noah reached across the table and gently placed his hands on top of mine. His voice lowered; he was more serious now than he had been all day.

"This is truly an amazingly kind offer. I thank you ... and I thank God for it."

I threw a small stack of bills on the table, and before I knew it, we were out in the street, walking the twelve blocks up Central Park

West toward the sanctuary I called home. The night was dark, and the cold rain stung my face, but I was glowing like a warm spring day. Noah walked briskly next to me. No words were spoken between us. The walk was over in a blink, and just about ten minutes later, I broke the plane of my home with Noah, an old, dirty homeless man I had met in the park just hours ago.

Noah paused to look about my magnificent apartment. His faced changed dramatically, displaying an awe and innocence like that of a young child. An incredible sight, no doubt, for a man that made his home in the open air of Central Park. His hesitation was hardly noticeable compared to the catastrophic set of negative predictions I now began to obsess over. I distanced myself from Noah; desperately, I fought back violent urges to prevent this filthy man from infecting the purity of my inner sanctum.

"Let's get you out of those clothes," I said, corralling Noah toward the guest bath without actually physically touching him.

Noah reached out toward me, and I instinctually darted past his touch.

"You seem distracted, nervous. Is everything okay?"

"I'm sorry. I am nervous, full of anxiety, actually. You must understand, I've never brought a complete stranger to my home," I said, corralling him toward the guest bath.

Noah contemplated the situation briefly.

"You know," he started in a soothing voice, "there are no strangers. There are just people, and we can choose to make them guests, or we can choose to perpetually distance ourselves from them. And as you know, it's fear that drives distance between people. And you are a most gracious host, focused on the comfort and wellbeing of your guest over your own sense of comfort and wellbeing. Your hospitality tonight can change the course of a man."

Noah paused at the bathroom door and turned back to me. "Quite possibly, it could change the course of humanity." And with that, he shut the door behind him.

I stood there for several minutes longer. More than once, I intended to barge in on him and demand he explain further. But when I heard the shower water running, I abandoned my confusion for the moment and turned to gather the things I suspected he would need.

It didn't take long for Noah to emerge into the grand room where I had taken up residence in one of the deep leather chairs next to the small fire I had started just minutes ago. He was wearing my clothes, which were a bit tight on his larger frame, but had to be far more comfortable than the filthy mess he had been wearing that was now in a crumpled pile somewhere in my home. I gestured to the large leather sofa near me with my right hand, which was tightly gripping a fresh glass of bourbon. Noah obliged and lay comfortably upon it, snuggling deeply into several of the large Egyptian cotton blankets that surrounded him. We enjoyed the absolute silence, disturbed only by an occasional crackle and pop from the fire. It was me that broke the peace at last.

"What did you mean I could change the course of humanity? I mean really, what does that mean?"

Noah looked deep into the fire. The light from the hearth cast soft, glowing shadows upon his face, making it appear more pious than I had noticed before. He took in a large, cleansing breath and let go a flood of words that moved me.

"Hospitality is a sacred expression of love for humanity, particularly when the fellowship between people is real. That is, when people are in no position to help each other in any way except spiritually, hospitality is a means to grow our faith. It enriches our perspective and extends our inherent connection with others in the world. It is through this act we find the fundamental building blocks of relationships, community, society, and faith. This is what allows us to be what we want to become."

Noah paused to let the words find their mark.

"Your kindness tonight is not the perverse act of climbing your corporate or social ladder, sharing your table in a calculated way with only those that can advance your temporal desires. Faith is not meant for when it's convenient, so don't distort it to shield against doing what is right or to justify inconsistencies or incongruities between His life, yours, or theirs."

I'm not sure I totally understood, but I thought about the infinite occasions I "wined and dined" in an effort to have my own selfish needs satisfied, manipulating clients, prospects, colleagues, friends of friends, and, of course, women. I gave and received hospitality for the sole purpose of advancing *my* cause or serving *my* needs.

"I can not make you a richer, more popular, or more powerful person. And you do not possess a single material item that I want."

Noah adjusted himself slightly on top of the firm sofa and beneath the soft blankets. Ironically, the level of comfort and grace he was now experiencing was somewhat uncomfortable for Noah.

"Hospitality is much more than providing food, drink, or even a place to rest one's head ..." he paused and let out a great yawn, " ... and to a *stranger*, for that matter."

His words became faint as he closed his eyes and retreated further into the comfort of the sofa.

"Listening to the hearts of people, understanding their nature, their situation, their hopes and dreams: that is the soul of compassion and a key ingredient to understanding your own place in the world. Yet we go on stuffing ourselves every day with as much stuff as we can fit in our packed and busy lives, rarely thinking at all about those that need us most. We have so much more than we need, and to share just a little can change the course of a man and humanity itself. And that is what you did tonight."

And with that, there was silence. The fire was burning low, and by the look of it, Noah's fire was out for the night. I rose slowly and looked down upon this sleeping heap, pausing to reflect on the extraordinary events of the day. As he lay asleep, seemingly deep in the grip of slumber, I turned to leave the room. As Noah began to fade in the darkness behind me, I heard one last declaration from beneath the blankets.

"Good things happened today," the words were faint, floating in the night.

"Huh?" I said peering in from halfway down the hallway.

He whispered as if talking in his sleep, "Good things happened today. And you were a big part of it."

I paused momentarily as the words had difficulty finding an understandable place in my mind, and then they disappeared from my thoughts altogether.

"Good night, Noah," I said and headed to bed. What was I going to do with Noah? Clearly, he needed help, but he was not a lost dog I found in the park. I drifted off to sleep with my mind racing, anxiously sorting through my options for tomorrow. But once my soul was at rest, I slept peacefully that night, like never before, and I dreamed of balance.

To be perfectly honest, I had not expected to find Noah. Certainly not this day, and certainly not in the way I did. But I would learn later that I did not find Noah; he found me, and he changed my life.

Chapter 4

Anna had no idea what she was doing. Then again, Anna rarely knew what she was doing. Eager to have this random experience fulfill some unmet need in her life, without thinking, she took the next exit and maneuvered the little Jetta back south on I-80. Her heart was full of wonder and excitement, and her mind was focused on the task at hand. Both were betrayed occasionally by logic, but fatefully, the betrayal was fleeting. In that moment, Anna committed to this like she had never committed to anything before. She was going home.

Home. Anna knew little about this concept since she had been running from her family for so long. The very thought of going home gave her great anxiety. Anna felt anger. Betrayal. Not for having been sent away at such a young age—she now saw that as a tremendously positive influence in her life—but because she resented the fact that her parents never came back for her. Somewhere deep within herself, Anna had always expected them to show up in California and throw themselves at her mercy, repenting for all their transgressions against her. Mostly, though, Anna just wanted to be rescued from the loneliness and isolation she had imparted on herself as a result.

As the years wore on, her anticipation turned to disappointment, and her disappointment ultimately turned to bitterness. For years, she hated her parents for not reuniting with her. But the past couple of years left her missing their connection, and the last couple of months left her thinking about a trip home, driven by her overwhelming desire to reconcile with those she loved and that loved her and to find her permanent place in the world.

Today, Noah was the catalyst that moved those powerful feelings that already existed into action. Once again, Anna was full of anticipation. She was full of hope. Somehow, this was the right time and place for her to head back to New Orleans. She was going home. At least, that's what she thought.

They were now a little over eight hours into their journey, fast approaching the Arizona border as the sun started to set behind them. As the little Jetta carrying its payload emerged over the slightest easement, Anna briefly glanced into her rearview mirror, then nearly lost her breath as she took in the brilliant display splashed across the sky behind her. Feeling the confinement of the small mirror, like some limited viewfinder that restricted the full beauty of her desire, Anna instinctually pulled the car over to the dusty shoulder and immediately popped the Jetta door open. Looking behind her, Anna stood in wonder on the Arizona highway. The irony did not escape her. Anna never looked back. But this view was magnificent.

At first, she couldn't even discern the difference between the millions of brilliant colors splashed across the sky or the vastness in which they stretched across the horizon. But after several minutes of observation, Anna could see it all. Sure, she felt so insignificant, but for the first time in her life, she knew she was a true part of the world. Leaning down and sticking her head back inside the car, she couldn't believe the old man was sleeping through this great epiphany within her own life.

"Noah," she said quietly at first. Then louder, "Noah, look!"

Noah stirred, slowly at first, then with greater excitement as he took in the scene. His awakening was nothing compared to that which he was about to witness.

"Sure is beautiful," he said, craning his neck and adjusting his old black hat, eyes affixed on the brilliant mixture of creation before them, unbuckling his seatbelt and letting himself into the warm Arizona evening, awash with the warm and generous flow of this gifted moment. "God is most amazing!" His hands were outstretched toward the dazzling display as he moved to the back of the car.

Anna's own disposition changed immediately with the thought of a greater power orchestrating this moment, or any other for that matter. Her body language was the traitor within, and Noah recognized the intrusion and responded in kind.

"Anna, what is it? This is a great and glorious moment; what are you afraid of? What are you running from?"

"Nothing," was her reaction. "Let's go," she said, moving toward the little car.

Noah, sensing the restlessness, took the issue head on.

"Please, come here," he said waving one hand toward himself while resting the rest of his weight against the trunk of the slightly overheated Jetta.

Anna paused. Noah was incredibly disarming. She immediately let her guard down and within seconds found herself resting her body near his, their fingers interlocking in a strong, but caring embrace, the awesome presence obviously still present.

Several minutes of silence passed as the two rediscovered the moment.

"Be careful," he started again with a slight, reassuring squeeze of his hand on hers. "Hoping your life will be longer because of the speed in which you live it is a dangerous course. You'll miss a great deal always running straight ahead, focused on moving too fast toward the end."

Anna didn't respond. Crushed under the burden of her own thoughts, she only watched the scene slowly extinguish in front of them, or behind them, depending on your perspective. Noah recognized this.

"On one hand," Noah started, choosing his words carefully, "the saltwater guppy swims over a million miles in its life, but never leaves a plot of sea that is more than twenty yards squared. That is a tremendous amount of activity for a very small fish in a very small space contained within a very, very vast ocean."

Anna couldn't piece together the point Noah was making. She listened intently as he continued.

"On the other hand, a betta fish might live in a gallon of water and occasionally swim from one side of the bowl to the other side. That fish has nowhere else to go."

Still, no formidable point formed in Anna's mind.

"And further," he continued, "the arctic tern flies some twenty thousand miles in one sitting so it can be home to breed and raise its young."

Anna looked puzzled. Noah got to the point.

"The gift and ability of exploration and experience can improve your understanding of the world, those in it, and your place among them. But ultimately, you are meant to be near those closest to you. There is no stronger foundation than relationship and community. It's from this source you can build a powerful and meaningful life."

Anna thought about her own "exploration and experience" over the past ten years but quickly recognized it as profane. Anna was always moving; that she was sure of. But she was always moving away from the parts of her life she perceived to be unpleasant and sometimes terrible. She never moved toward that which mattered to her most. In that moment, she recognized the significance of the subtle difference.

It was now much darker. The sun had all but set, the brilliant colors reduced to a more muted blue-gray, with a low-laying orange glow. It was quiet, too. Anna and Noah returned to the contained interior of the small, black Jetta. The key turned, the engine started, and they were once again headed east. And they were headed *toward* something, something that mattered to both of them deeply. It was clear to Noah. It was not so clear to Anna. Not yet.

Not a word was spoken between them as the small Jetta rattled across the Arizona highway, the small headlights illuminating only a short distance in front of them. Anna thought about their sunset discussion and what it meant to her. Noah thought about Anna. Finally, Noah broke the silence

"Anna."

"Yes?" she said in the form of a question, her head turned slightly toward him, but her eyes did not leave the small patch of radiance on the road that was now guiding them through the dark desert.

"I noticed you became quite uneasy earlier when I glorified God."

Anna immediately shifted uneasily in her seat. Her balance was now broken over a topic that confused her commendably.

"That's exactly what I mean," he continued pointing at her reaction. "Anna, do you not believe in God?"

Noah let the long and uncomfortable pause hang in the air, expanding upon its own energy until it filled the entire car, eventually squeezing an answer out of Anna.

"I don't know what I believe. I want to believe, but I just don't know. I would prefer some concrete evidence, some actual proof, you know."

"Ah. I see," came the quick reply. Noah adjusted himself in his seat so that most of his frame was now pointing toward her. "I guess the reality is we don't know *exactly*—God's height, weight, location … His purpose. And while I suppose the pursuit of knowing is admirable, it shouldn't be at the expense of faith."

"That's not exactly what I meant by proof. I would settle for some logical rationale of His existence."

"Really? Did you mean something more like Thomas Aquinas' attempt to quantify God through teleological argument in his

Quinquae Viae, or *Five Proofs of God?* Why do we do that? It's ironic, isn't it?"

"Do what?"

"The fact that we try and prove or disprove everything in our world with science, with manmade concepts like math or physics, even the existence of God. And yet, using paint or words or feelings to prove His existence is ridiculed. The world is ironic, and irony has no bounds. Maybe God is irony, or at least ironic."

Anna listened, and she hoped. She hoped that Noah might inspire a new perspective, to give life where it was barren, to pour light into a room that had remained shrouded in darkness for so long.

"And, of course, there have been others. For example, a man name Dembrosky, in an attempt to prove the act of Creation, and therefore the existence of God, created the concept of *specified complexity* where anything with less than a 1 in 10^{150} chance of occurring naturally in the world was impossible. That, ironically, was rejected by mainstream scientists, even though most physicists use a much smaller statistic, 1 in 10^{41}, as the criteria for determining when something is out of the realm of possibility, at least when conveniently applied as scientific rigor to a process or application they want to prove or deny. Yet others, like Dr. Coppedge, have calculated the probability of forming 238 proteins together, the very minimal combination needed to sustain the most simplistic forms of life on Earth, would be something on the scale of 1 in $10^{29,345}$."

Anna had been down this path before, at Berkley. She took a series of theology classes in hopes of sorting out her own chaotic belief system. And from that experience, she responded with some sense of confidence, although because she had hoped for more, she delivered the counterpoint from a point of disappointment.

"Sure, but like John Allen Paulos has argued, just because something is highly improbable, even approaching impossible, it doesn't mean it can't actually happen. His simple point about being dealt thirteen specific cards in a friendly hand of bridge is statistically 1 in 600 billion. And regardless of how impossible the random assembly of those cards is, we get them each time we play the game."

"Paulos? Never heard of him. Sounds like another maniacally egotistical mind that can envision no power greater than his own, or even the collective of human ingenuity. My point is deeper, Anna. No one can scientifically prove or disprove the existence of God. In fact, no one can scientifically prove or disprove that I loved my wife and children and would have given my life for them. But the fact indelibly remains that I loved them infinitely and would gladly have given my life for them. Love is unscientific, but I think you would agree that it exists, that is has purpose, and that it has a profound impact on the world we live in."

Wife? Children? Past tense. This sidetracked Anna's thoughts momentarily, but Noah had launched into a passionate soliloquy, and Anna wanted desperately to provide him an attentive audience. She decided to wait and come back to this when the time was right.

"The fact that God, or God's actions, are not observable, repeatable or falsifiable, that God's very existence violates the manmade principle of parsimony is utterly absurd. Only that which can be seen and understood is real or true. What egos we must have! It's pathetic how we try to explain our supernatural gifts with our human faculties, creating and applying science with our inherently limited abilities. Aren't we so maniacally egotistical to think there is no greater power or intelligence? How can you believe the feelings that overwhelm us when experiencing a sunrise or sunset, a gentle breeze or an infant's touch are nothing more than chemical reactions in a carbon coating? Do you really believe we are just well-organized monkeys?" Noah's voice was building.

"What's the point of your action or insight? It's hard for me, a man of limited intelligence, to ignore the amazing beauty and perfection of the machinery that orchestrates our existence each day. It is staggering to me. Broadly speaking, I mean the cycles of life and death, the procession of seasons, the evolution of life, including the tiny subset we know as humanity. I marvel in my own inept way at the most incredible, brilliant, beautifully designed systems reaching complexity of unimaginable proportions. More precisely, I mean the wondrous design of millions and billions of chance events occurring in sequence each day to bring about perfect order to our world, even if it's surrounded in chaotic complexity. It's illogical to think that atoms, throughout infinite time, suddenly and without thought, accidentally came together in order to create extraordinary order, chaos, consciousness, and intelligence. Did you know every human being spends about half an hour as a single cell, and then somehow that single cell multiplies and divides using the same material it originally started out as, but somehow intelligently directs groups of same cell formations to part from the pack, and to start organizing in their own unique and complex forms and groupings to develop vastly different forms and functions like the heart, lungs, liver, brain, and skin. The human brain alone has over 100 billion neurons working in a coordinated manner to form images, words, thoughts, and feelings." Noah's voice was reaching a crescendo.

"That alone is miraculous, and yet it's but a grain of sand on the beach. And still we want to explain the unexplainable with simple, manmade concepts like *enormous selection pressure* which seems so … so … well, it just seems so absurd!"

Anna reached over and placed her hand upon his knee. Noah responded with a deep gaze in her direction. He pulled in a deep, deep breath and let it go with relief. He paused for a moment, then started again, slowly, quietly, more deliberately.

"Great thinkers throughout time—Plato, Aristotle and even Cicero—contemplated the idea that there was someone, or something, far greater than humanity that intelligently designed a system beyond our comprehension. Even today, our greatest thinkers concede the actual point of creation lies outside the scope of presently known levels of science and that we must therefore leave open the possibility that God exits."

Anna was moved by Noah's passion. His arguments were sound, logical. But they failed to penetrate her highly fortified skepticism.

"God exists," Noah continued in a calm and deliberate way, "but that concept is too great for us to begin to understand. We know next to nothing about the universe we live in, and if space is infinite, we have not even explored ourselves fully, much less begun to truly understand anything about who we are and why we are here. I understand we want to prove God's existence and make sense of our own, to anchor our place in the world and within the universe. To do so is good. But we too often ask the wrong questions, like 'Why are we here and where did we come from?' Or, 'Does God exist?' These are important questions for sure, but the pursuit of knowledge must take us beyond these selfish concerns and into the realm of constructing a common understanding of what God wants for us and wants us to be. I accept outright God exists, and truly I say to you, we are reflections of a more pure existence. So our perceived reality afforded to us by language, art, math, science, and other means of reflecting the reflection is all meta-art that allows us to construct a reality within the context of our own limitations. And only when each and every one of us embraces this profound truth and wipes away the dirt and grime gathered throughout time, obstacles that distort a truer reflection of a greater presence, a larger existence, will we have answers to our most profound questions."

No more words were spoken. At least an hour passed as the two traveled across Arizona and toward New Mexico. Anna thought deeply about Noah's words. They held great meaning and relevance to her, even though she did not fully understand all of them. But for the first time in her own life, Anna had hope for faith. And yet, something different kept emerging at the forefront of her thoughts. Something that demanded a question even though it might not have an answer. At last, she could wait no longer.

"Noah?"

"Yes, Anna."

"What was your wife's name?"

Noah's expression changed immediately, dramatically. He quickly turned away from Anna and looked far out into the Arizona desert. He disappeared in his own thoughts for a long, long time. Anna waited patiently for him, delicately, not pressing the issue in the slightest way. It was clear to her the topic was taboo.

"Anna," Noah finally broke the quiet silence with one word.

"Yes, Noah."

"No, I mean her name was Anna."

Chapter 5

I awoke to find Noah in the kitchen. He was sitting quietly, staring out my leaded glass windows that overlooked 70th Street. He had the newspaper in front of him, which was entirely intact except for the classifieds section that had been surgically removed and placed on the opposite end of the small breakfast table. A whisp of steam periodically floated out of the cup of cappuccino sitting untouched in front of him.

"Good morning," I said softly, concerned with interrupting the quiet trance Noah seemed to be indulging in.

He turned slowly and looked at me. His serious, somber face evaporated and was replaced with a large, bright, happy look.

"It is a wonderful morning," he said back to me.

I spoke no words as I made myself a double espresso. The desire was more for the taste than the need as my mind, my body, and my soul were wide awake, and my senses were in overdrive. I was excited for the day. I had no idea what to expect, and that excited me. For the first time in my life, I craved to convert the unknown, to make it known to me, instead of being frozen in fear by its presence.

I looked up occasionally as the coffee machine whined, whirred, and whistled only to find Noah had returned to his windows—my windows—and the activity on West 70th Street below.

I took a seat at the small breakfast table with the classifieds in front of me.

"Were you looking for something?" I asked, moving my eyes toward the paper.

Noah's view met mine on the table, and the smile immediately returned to his face.

"Nothing in particular. I just like to look."

"Look at what?"

"All of the things there that will change lives today, tomorrow, or next week."

My puzzled look demanded further clarification.

"You know," he continued, "jobs, dates, cars that carry them away, knickknacks that they bring home."

"Oh," I said, pulling the paper closer. Reading the words now, I saw how they transformed people's lives. I had never thought of the classifieds in that way. Of course, I had never really thought of anything in that way, but the curiosity was certainly there. And as I scanned the page looking at nothing, and for nothing, another strange twist of fate revealed itself from the ethereal.

"I saw it, too," Noah said looking deep into my soul.

"Saw what?"

"The 1950 Panhead Harley Chopper," he said turning his lethal gaze back to the streets below. "Let's go look at it today."

"How did you ... I can't." I said responding instinctually. "I have to get to work."

Noah turned his gaze back on me. No words.

I glanced back down at the paper, took a strong gulp of the stronger espresso, and considered the offer.

"No," came my rational judgment, and I again shook my head quickly. "It's all the way in Connecticut. I've already missed a day of work ... and they are expecting me. No way."

Noah smiled and confidently placed both of his strong and weathered hands on the table, interlocking his fingers while almost hugging his coffee.

"But you've already broken the chain, my friend. See how far it takes you," he said, his knowing smile already in front of my ultimate decision.

I stared, puzzled at this insane idea, this insane man. Was I insane?

"Besides," he continued, "it is a glorious day outside ... and it is a 1950 Panhead Harley after all." Noah emphasized this point with a little gesture toward the paper.

"There's no way. I don't have time." My words were an obvious and final ultimatum without reserve. This insanity had to end, and my work, my life, beckoned for me to return.

"Time?" Noah replied in a confused, almost disdainful tone. "Time is nothing more than a clever parlor trick humanity has invented to convince some there is not enough of it, or to remind others, like me, there is too much of it."

I was stunned.

"The reality is," Noah said after a long moment, allowing me to struggle with the thought he knew I could not absorb. "the reality is, no matter how we look at it, there is just the right amount of time for each us; we just have to know the right way to spend it."

I pushed back from the table and stepped toward the window. A beautiful early spring morning was indeed emerging from under the dark, cold night. My thoughts were affixed on the meeting I *needed* to lead in just a couple of hours.

My thoughts wandered away from this compulsion and over to a simpler, more necessary set of concerns. This could be just the type of activity I needed to diffuse my growing sense of urgency and restlessness. Obviously, I couldn't live the rest of my life with Noah, but I wanted to be sure I helped give him a lift and that we could part amicably, which meant me feeling good about leaving him behind. The trip would give me time to think about how to get Noah the help he needed while recapturing my life, my routine.

"Yeah, okay," I finally said, "let's go take a look."

"Excellent, then it's settled," he said relaxing back in his chair. "Let's have some toast and maybe an orange or a banana, then be on our way."

And so it was. Just like that, we were in a taxi headed for Grand Central Station.

"It's me," I said curtly, watching Manhattan stream by from my cab window. It was always flying by in a cartoon sense of way, like when I was a child pretending the entire world was an animated scene that I could jump into without a thought.

"I won't be in today. I have a ... ," I paused and turned to Noah, who looked like a small child staring back at me, as if he were grasping for a handle on the moment.

"I have a personal issue to take care of today," I paused and listened.

"Yes. Everything is fine. Don't worry. I will be in tomorrow."

I flipped the phone closed and imagined the catastrophic chain reaction that was just ignited, then purposely powered my iPhone off altogether. The course was set. There was no turning back. I could allow no interruptions.

Minutes later, we found ourselves standing in a long line at the Metro North ticket counter in Grand Central Station. Hundreds of voices simultaneously bounced and echoed throughout the great hall, then found partnership with the slapping of wooden shoes moving countless numbers of apprehensive people quickly across the marble floors. The sounds intermingled to create an incomprehensible message of caution only outdone by the occasional intercom announcement, "7:25 Stamford Express is boarding on Track 121." And finally it was our turn.

"Two round trip tickets to Stamford," I said without even looking at the woman behind the window.

"That's wrong!" snapped Noah, immediately slamming an open palm on the cash I was attempting to shove through the small space between the open window and the granite counter.

"I am not coming back, and besides ..." he calmed down a bit while lifting his hand from over mine after noticing my obvious concern, "and anyways, you can always buy return tickets later at the station, or even on the train back," he said with a gentle smile.

"So you're staying in Stamford?" I questioned uneasily, but with great optimism.

"Yes."

"Do you have family there?"

"Something like that," Noah finished the debate with another glacier stare.

"Sir!" came the curt quip from the rugged, young Italian woman from behind the thick glass, her voice escaping more from under the pass-through than the intercom built into the glass.

"Give me a one-way ticket and a round-trip ticket to Stamford please." Noah looked disappointed.

"There's an express train leaving in five minutes from track 121, downstairs. You'll need to hurry."

"Thanks," I said, grabbing my change and our tickets, and I quickly turned to hurry across the crowded and bustling terminal toward the stairs leading down to track 121.

The conductor held the sliding door for another ten seconds after seeing the last few passengers hurrying toward the train. Noah and I were among them, and we slipped past him and onto the car at the last possible moment.

"Thank you, sir," Noah said, recognizing the extra bit of care, however small, the conductor extended to us by holding the train a few seconds beyond its scheduled departure time in order for us to board. This appreciation, of course, went totally unnoticed, or at least ignored, by the conductor himself.

We found plenty of seats on this northbound train, and this car in particular was for the most part empty as the majority of the business commuters that were onboard had chosen to move forward to the first or second cars in order to get the edge on everyone else by being closer to the terminal exits upon reaching their final destination. Also, most of the Metro area was coming southbound into the city at this early morning hour, anyway. We were "reverse commuting" at this time, which few people did.

I took a seat next to the window and faced forward. Noah chose to sit directly across from me, his back facing the forward motion of the train, and while I looked directly into his eyes, he cocked his head to the right and stared out the window, waiting patiently for the trip to begin.

Within seconds, the train lurched forward and began to slowly twist and turn though the dark, ominous tunnels under the bustling streets of New York. The iron wheels wrestled the metal track beneath, producing the constant screech and scream of metal on metal while occasionally throwing off a dazzling burst of blue fluorescent sparks, illuminating a shadowy steel column or a lonely doorway to nowhere.

Looking out the window during this part of the trip proved to be useless as the interior lights shining against the tinted windows in the absolute darkness of the underground track produced a mirror effect inside the train. Except for when the sparks flew, staring out the window had you staring into your own reflection, and Noah seemed to enjoy this because he remained statuesque, staring intensely at the window.

My mind wandered away from my own reflection and on to the ridiculous décor of the train. Fake leather seats in red and blue. At least this car was new and the seats were clean. The few people that sat around us were settling in for the trip ahead—an old couple beside us, a woman and her young daughter to the back and left of us, a business man standing in the breezeway.

My observation of those around me was short lived, and I was drawn almost immediately back to my reflection in the window. I stared at my own face for a moment, falling into a sort of hypnotic state. And before long, I was looking past my external appearance and a little deeper into my own soul; I didn't really like what I saw.

Physically, I was certainly not harmful to the eyes. But this glass reflected more. At first, I caught only a glimpse of the lesions that covered my heart, or maybe it was my soul. The momentary revelation was initially shocking to me, approaching appalling, and I gasped initially, but with time, I became entranced in the horror that stared back at me. My facial features vanished in the dark, tinted window, and a ghastly realization appeared in its place. As I raised my hand to feel if my face was even still there, there was a violent jerk of the train, and a blast of brilliant light incinerated the image. We had emerged into the open, outside landscape of the raised track just over 125th Street, and just like that, I was catapulted back into my living reality.

Noah shot up in his seat, pushing his face even closer to the window.

"It is a beautiful day," he said in a big voice through an even bigger smile. He never once turned his gaze in my direction.

I, however, was jarred from what I could only assume was some sort of panic-induced hallucination, or at least that's what I rationalized what had just happened to me. A quick uneasy glance around the car led me to believe I looked as normal as I always did; no one reacted any differently. The small, young child sitting only a few rows away actually smiled at me as we made eye contact. Still, while I struggled to emerge from my panic, the symptoms of this attack intensified within me. My hands were clammy and slightly damp from the sweat, and my heart raced uncontrollably like it wanted to escape through my chest. I felt lightheaded and was actually gasping slightly for air as I smothered myself with my own profane thoughts.

"Relax," Noah said, rescuing me from myself with a gentle hand on my knee and a simple suggestion. "Enjoy this day. Enjoy this company. Enjoy this experience. Be here with me as I am here with you. It is good for me. It is good for you. It is good for the world."

Noah turned back to the landscape outside that raced inescapably past us across the large train window. "It makes me think about one of my favorite Psalms," he continued in a gentle, nurturing way. Now his eyes were closed as he whispered:

> "O God, just as we look into a mirror to see any soiled spots on our face,
> let us look to you to understand the things that we have done astray.
> We are like a reed shaking in the wind.
> We are inexpressibly weak.
> Leave us not to ourselves,
> but dwell in our hearts and guide our thoughts and actions."

My anxiety evaporated as if Noah had just opened the door to a hot steam bath and all of the humid, oppressive air was sucked immediately from the room.

Noah looked back at me, his huge brown eyes heavy with the weight of that which they had seen over the years.

"Thank you, Noah," I said, trying in some way to convey my deep gratitude for his ability to overwhelm my senseless thoughts of anxiety and static with important thoughts of life and balance.

"Thank *you*," was all he said at first, then he continued with something more profound. "It's really quite simple."

"What is?" I asked, shifting slightly in my seat, and leaning forward into Noah's words.

"Faith. Balance. Peace. Most of it starts with the simple gift of observation."

"Observation?" I was intrigued.

"Yes. Observation." He said it so definitively, as if it were an absolute. "Our ability to perceive is an extraordinary gift given to us directly from God to experience the world around us, the world in which we live, the people with whom we live. Observation is our means of understanding and fulfillment, yet we feel compelled to fill our moments and hours, day after day until our lives are over, with the static of manic impulses and stimulation which does nothing but obscure our true observational gifts. And I mean all of them, not just those we rely on most."

Noah just described me fundamentally, and he was not done yet.

"Try spending a day intensely focused on sensing the world around you simultaneously through all of your senses, truly experiencing the sights and sounds around you while focused especially on the smells associated with certain instances and the taste that is subtly masking itself in the background. Touch, our most powerful gift, is often held hostage to the dictators of sight and sound, but has the power to heal most of our wounds. And don't forget your emotional senses. Have you ever tapped into these to truly understand people around you? The reality is you'll never see anything relying solely on what your eyes can see."

Noah paused. We sat staring at one another. Noah was obviously anticipating something from me, but my puzzled face forced him to urge me further.

"Go ahead."

"With what?"

Noah was slightly annoyed at my resistance.

"I want you to take in the things around you using all the observational gifts at your disposal."

I immediately turned around and scanned the entirety of the train car.

"No, no, no," Noah said gently shaking his head. "Face forward a moment, find a place on my face to focus on; have you done it? Now, forget about what you see, and open your other senses to the experience that is now. Feel the weight of your feet on the floor below, feel the floor pushing back up against your feet. Feel the weight of your hips being suspended by the seat you're in. Feel your place in the world settle with each breath."

Noah's words drifted to the background as I focused on the totality of my experience here and now. I could feel my feet connecting to the floor below, and I could feel the weight of my body being suspended by the chair. I could feel my body being gently pressed deeper into the cushion as the train accelerated north toward Stamford. As these senses intensified, I added others, like the fairly strong aroma of several different coffees intermingling and finding its way to my olfactory receptors. It was comforting, and I could nearly taste their deliciousness as they mixed with the lip balm I had applied to my dry, cracking lips earlier that morning. Noah had stopped speaking, so I listened intently for other sounds that could be added to my experience. Pushing the loud "clack, clack" of the train to the background, I focused on fine tuning the chatter coming from within the cabin. In particular, the sweet, gentle voice of a child playing pretend in the seats nearby.

I was totally in the moment, and my senses were working together harmoniously in a way they had never before. I was experiencing my life in a way I had never before. And *now* I was ready to look around. Slowly, I shifted my gaze away from Noah's face, which was now filled with a quiet, content expression, and again I *observed* the other people in the cabin, the lives that lived around me. There was a young mom, neatly dressed and doting over that young girl playing quietly next to her. Emotionally connected, the young mother briefly smiled in my direction. I smiled back. She turned to her daughter and the smile grew larger.

An old man and his old wife were also nearby. They were sitting tightly together as I imagined they had for the last fifty years or more. Neither noticed me. There old hands weakly clasped but held on as tightly as they could so as not to lose one another as they hurled down the tracks of life.

A young man stood stiffly in the breezeway and talked incessantly on his cell phone. He reminded me of me, except his face seemed more thoughtful; he was more connected to the world around him than I ever even pretended to be.

I was far more relaxed now. Noah smiled knowingly and again turned his attention to the day that had blossomed into an experience. And as I began to join Noah in a quiet appreciation of the life that flowed within us and around us, the train jerked around the bend, sending the old woman's Louis Vuitton bag tumbling from her lap to the floor, its contents fleeing the captivity of the purse with the same enthusiasm as a prison riot.

The young man in the breezeway sprang into action.

"Gotta go," was all he said before snapping the phone shut and kneeling to the floor. "I've got it. I've got it," he assured her as he dutifully collected her bag, lipstick, a pack of tissues, glasses and about eighty seven cents of change.

"Here you are, ma'am," was all he said before retreating back to the breezeway and once again flipped his phone open. But before the little old lady could even respond, the young girl appeared over the seat from behind her.

"Here you go," she said, her small, soft voice barely audible, and her hand was outstretched, holding a small prescription bottle, for glaucoma as it would turn out. And just about the same time a bright red, rubber ball rolled quickly toward me, then came to a rest against my large, black boot. I leaned over slowly, picked up the ball, and handed it gently back to her.

"Thank you, dear," she said genuinely, reaching her hand toward mine. Oceans of blue filled her eyes in a way that expressed the vast and deep legacy she had left the world with.

"It's for my grandson," she continued, "we are on our way to see him now."

"It's infectious," Noah broke into the moment.

"What is?" My senses remained acutely aware, but I retreated to the more dominant sense of sight and sound as I focused back on Noah.

"The inherent nature of kindness. It's infectious, and it has the ability to spread quickly. But evil, while unnatural, can spread just as quickly if left unchecked. But people are inherently good; our entire social balance proves that fact."

I thought about the magnitude of that statement. Sure, there were bad people in the world. But I also believed people generally wanted to help before they wanted to hurt. In my own little corner of the world, I could see millions of people converge on New York City, and while it only took a few to cause massive pain and disruption—and occasionally that was the case—more often than not, good reigned over evil. We just don't see it on the news every day. I chuckled as I thought to myself, "Man on train goes out of his way to help little old lady pick up her belongings—little girl helps out—details at 11:00." But then my thought went further. Maybe someone should start a news channel that reported nothing but good deeds—no matter how small— and conscious acts of kindness. It could be called "Good Things Happened Today" or something like that. Anyone and everyone could be a contributing reporter.

"But the real question is how do we explain its existence?" Noah continued his original stream of thought.

"What?" I asked for some reason, as if I didn't hear the original question. Why do we always do that?

"I mean, how do you prefer to explain your life and the lives being lived around you?"

I so immensely enjoyed being with Noah but clearly lagged far behind his own thinking. I had no idea what I was doing or where this would lead, but I knew I was here with Noah now, and I was intensely enjoying the moment. But, once again, I had no idea what Noah was talking about.

"What's better to explain the world and our lives here in it?" he repeated the same question in a slightly different way. "Art or science? I myself am conflicted. What do you think?"

Once again Noah's eyes sliced through mine with an ethereal sense of knowledge.

My blank stare was all the prompt Noah needed, and after only a minute or two, he continued leading the discussion.

"I happen to be attracted to the acts of literature, specifically, and the arts generally. Science, while an incredibly useful tool that man has created, has yet to come close to explaining, or even reflecting, the important aspects of life or the world we live in, particularly the things that matter most. The bond between a man and his wife, for example, or the feelings they have for their children much less. A gentle breeze, a gentle kiss, or a love that usurps both. And while any pursuit of understanding the human condition is most admirable, science seems to pursue answers to how we exist as we do, while music, literature, art, and philosophy seemingly seek the answers to why we exist as we do."

Now I thought I understood.

"That's not exactly true," I started my response. "Science can tell us exactly why the sun comes up in the morning, why the body gets sick or why it gets better. It is science that has unlocked the very deepest of secrets our universe has kept shrouded from us for eons."

I was quite pleased with my position, and Noah seemed to agree, which gave me a confidence to push on.

"Just think about the impact science has had on our way of life. It is science that provides the ability to travel into space, insights into how our bodies work, the ability to cure cancer." I emphasized the last phrase with a quick raise of my eyebrows to further demonstrate the great and powerful good science brings to humanity.

"Yes. All of that is true. But my point is more about strengthening the underlying fabric that directs our passions and how we apply the tools we have created with our limited capacity and understanding and to what ideals we apply them. Most importantly, we need to foster an environment and society that values the enduring nature of art, philosophy, and theology, as well as other academic and spiritual pursuits so we can value the individual human, the state of humanity, and the drive for understanding and improving the collective good—over money, power, or other material gain."

I instinctually smirked at this idealistic utopia Noah was rambling about.

"That's a kind thought, Noah, but where is the practical reality in a world so dependent on material gain for even our basic needs like food and shelter?"

My question was sincere. At least my belief in my question was.

Noah sighed. Not a heavy sigh, but it was enough to let me know he was disappointed.

"I've known many of the wealthiest and most powerful people in the world to be absolute dolts. Well educated academically, but idiots, blind to what really matters."

Noah rubbed his hands together intensely as he scooted closer to me. His right hand now tightly clenched my left shoulder, forcing me to look at him directly. His eyes were locked with mine.

"Understand yourself along with those around you and the world we live in together. Make it a better place now and for future generations. Otherwise, much like aerosols and emissions that will eat away at the ozone which protects our fragile existence from being destroyed by radiation, so, too, will apathy, greed, doubt, and disbelief drive purpose and meaning from our lives. These are the true fundamental building blocks of life protecting our fragile existence from extinction. The balance is dependent upon us. The system is fragile, so do your part to strengthen it, and just as importantly, do nothing to weaken it. Ultimately, the question for all times asks, 'Is the world a better place with me in it?' Your time and energy are finite, so expend them wisely. And that means always doing what's right, for others first, then yourself, even if that is to your disadvantage."

I thought about these words, which immediately stimulated thoughts of happier times in my life. Specifically, the nine months I spent working on a concrete construction crew between graduating from college and the start of my MBA work at one of the most prestigious colleges in the country. Several of the guys on the crew were college students, but most were lifelong concrete builders, either having built concrete structures all of their lives, or were young and just starting out, but destined to build concrete structures all their lives. Regardless, they were all well grounded and intensely focused on that which matters—their minds, their bodies, their friends, their families, and their faith. And while their lives could have taken them in any direction and placed them with any group of individuals, they were here, working and living together. It was a very tightly knit group. They cared a great deal for their work, but mostly they cared deeply for each other.

For me, that work started in December and ended in early September. During that time, the weather went from frigid, to cool and breezy, to stagnate and sweltering. Each day, I embraced the backbreaking manual labor. But the evenings I reserved for reading. gently swinging my exhausted muscles on the front porch swing, I devoured words from some of history's most critical thinkers like Aristotle, René Descartes, Hugh Blair, Karl Marx, Ayn Rand, Kenneth Burke, Stephen Toulmin, and so on.

The often silent and solitary work allowed me to think more broadly about their words and how they might apply to the world I lived in now—or not. At times, that thinking inevitably postured philosophical questions that were discussed and debated at great depths with my crew as we dug trenches for footers, bolted frames in place, tied rebar, poured concrete, and ripped our temporary frames from the concrete walls that would stand for years to come.

My heart and body strengthened through the labor required to build something enduring, something lasting like a road, a foundation for a home, or a retaining wall that would keep the elements from destroying a school's playground. That mindless manual labor was some of the most thought-provoking, spiritually-lifting, and enduring work I had ever done. And it never did, or never would, earn me the kind of money I wanted so I could get the things I wanted.

Creating ads made me a lot of money, but it pillaged my body, my mind, my heart, my soul, and my rightful place in the world. Not that making ads inherently did that, but certainly my pursuit of the wrong compensation contributed immensely to where I was and what I had become.

To this point, I had lived my life by a very specific creed, which I attributed in large part to what I had achieved so far. From an early age, I had taught myself to take a hard look at where I was, what I was doing, and who I surrounded myself with. I made that evaluation early and I made it often. Before today, the motivation for adhering to the creed was making me successful, and others were a necessary evil for making that happen. And while the creed would remain, my drive and motivation would now be inversed. What could I do to make the people around me happier, more successful, more fulfilled, and more connected to the world that we live in?

My eyes turned back to Noah. He was staring at me intensely with a joyful and fulfilling look covering his face. He smiled his knowing smile at me.

"Stamford, next stop!" screamed the conductor, breaking the sacred moment of my growing epiphany. The train screeched, then did a final lurch forward toward its resting place at Stamford Station. And just like that, I lurched back into my world but with a slightly different orientation.

Within seconds, Noah and I burst into the cool and refreshing morning air and onto the station platform, each of us coughing slightly as we tried to take in a large and fulfilling breath. It was nice to be outside, free from the confines of the city, and it was shaping up to be a beautiful day.

We estimated our destination to be within walking distance from the station, so we shunned the line of cabbies and cut due east across Atlantic Street. While the sun was shining higher in the sky now, we faced a slight headwind that made the day seem a bit colder than it actually was. Noah was walking at a determined pace. He seemed to know exactly where he was headed, so I followed without a word.

We cut through a vacant lot behind an old furniture store, and my comfortable surrounding quickly deteriorated around me. The buildings were getting more and more dilapidated, and the grunge seemed to pile higher with each step we took. Old tendencies emerged as we crossed Garden Street and into another lot. I noticed a small group of men huddled around a barrel. There were three or four of them, so my normal instincts moved me in the opposite direction. Noah, of course, did the opposite, and after a brief hesitation, I followed.

"How you all doin' today?" Noah greeted them loudly as if coming home after a long time away.

"You know, same old deal. Fighting off the cold ... and the hunger," the little guy closest responded without even looking up. The other three ignored his greeting altogether.

I stopped short of encroaching into their space and observed Noah communing with the group from a distance. The burning wood within the barrel gave off a pungent smell; the highway, mixed with an occasional train passing by, was creating a droning hum somewhere in the distance. My hands were stuffed deep and comfortably in my wool jacket pockets while the crisp wind continued to bite at my nose and cheeks. Noah was passing to each of the men something from his own jacket pockets: some loose change for one, an orange from my kitchen to another, and if I didn't know any better, I think he actually gave away his old, wool gloves, worn from a lifetime of extending a helping hand.

Noah brought that context to me. He was teaching me about living life for others. Noah didn't even know he existed except for the fact that he existed for others. He was a pink fish looking to help someone, searching to help anyone.

Satisfied, Noah headed back to me.

"Let's go, we're close now," he said pointing toward the next road over. Not another word.

A quick right on Pacific Street led us deeper into the rundown neighborhood. I was happy to be back on a sidewalk and out of the vacant lot, but my feet started to hurt with the grinding inside my boots on the cold, hard concrete. The walk was shaping up to be further than I thought. I kept my eyes focused on the ground in front of me, mostly to suppress any more sights that might ignite a full blown panic attack as my unfounded fear grew. In fact, concentrating on the dull pain in my left pinkie toe caused by the rubbing on the inside surface of my rigid black boot seemed to help offset the useless thoughts of fear and anxiety.

Looking up to be sure Noah was still with me, I couldn't believe my eyes. There it was. Its brilliant blue chassis was shining in the sunlight, further amplifying the glorious gleam of the powerful chrome-plated engine that bulged from under the fat, signature style gas tank. Its original solo saddle seat had been replaced with a classic black leather two-up seat, and the "ape hanger" handle bars had been lowered. I assumed both were done so that a couple could more comfortably drive longer distances. Regardless, it was stunning, and I was excited like a kid on Christmas morning. I was actually standing in the presence of a beautifully restored 1950 Panhead Harley.

Momentarily shaking off my awe-induced myopia, I stepped back from the elegant machine to take in my surroundings. We had ended up at a Harley-Davidson dealer located in a narrow, two-story brick building that I now noticed was sandwiched between a tattoo parlor and a homeless shelter.

A homeless shelter. My attention moved quickly back to Noah, who was smiling broadly, circling the Harley with an austere respect for its history and a playful giddiness for its potential. Things were adding up in my mind: the one-way ticket, the men in the lot, the ease of which Noah found this place, and the homeless shelter. It all made sense now. This had to be where Noah lived. And while that thought brought some temporary relief to me, I was saddened at the realization that my adventure would soon be over. My adventure would soon be replaced with my normal life … my work.

My work. That thought struck me like a lighting bolt. Instinctually, I shoved my hand into my jacket pocket, fishing around inside for my beloved iPhone. There it was. I gripped it, and a perverted comfort covered me momentarily. My morbid curiosity drove me further. Without thinking, I pressed the power button and waited for an instant.

Dang. Eight missed calls and two new voice messages. Looking at the call logs, it was easy to tell that the vast majority of them originated from my Madison Avenue office building. I glanced up at Noah, who was now heading inside, then pressed "get messages" on my phone. Turning my back to the Harley, I listened to the first desperate message.

"It's me. The place is going crazy. They're asking questions, you know. Questions I don't have answers to. Please call me. I hope everything is okay, but you have to help me. There is someone in front of me demanding answers every twenty minutes. Call me. Please."

My anxiety increased a bit, but I recognized this fear more as my "business performance adrenaline" than I did a destructive force in my life. That message was more of an irritant that a real concern. The next one wasn't so benign.

"Where the hell are you? We're just over a week away from one of the biggest pitches in this agency's history and you're totally MIA. Your career is riding on this, let me remind you. You can't afford to fuck this up; you'll never recover. I need to know you're all over this."

Dang. That was not my boss. Sure, I had a boss; everyone does. But with the talent I possessed, I was left to operate independently the majority of the time. But when things got heated, I took my direction from the guy that ran the entire company, and that was him.

I shoved the phone back into my pocket and spun around to see Noah emerging from within the dealership. What was I doing? I had to get back to New York, my office, my work, my life. I looked more closely toward Noah, who was quickly moving toward me, grinning broadly and shaking something at me. What did he have there? No.

"Let's take it for a drive!" he said, shoving the simple set of keys into my hands.

That thrilling prospect sent shivers through my body. But that impractical thought was instantly replaced with my reality.

"I can't, Noah. I just can't. I have to get back to New York. I have very important people counting on me to accomplish some very important things," I said extending the set of keys out back toward him.

Noah paused and looked briefly at the ground, then back to me.

"You have people right here counting on you to accomplish very important things."

I shook my head slightly.

"Noah, this is different. This is about what I do, what I need to do. And I have to go."

Noah stared at me, and I stared right back at Noah. We stared at each other for quite some time, each of us waiting for the other to make the first move.

"Doing something you don't enjoy is like imparting your own life sentence, as is doing the same thing for too long," Noah drew his weapon first. "We work to satisfy certain temporal needs, but more so to satisfy deep emotional needs associated with routine, order, accomplishment, fulfillment, challenge, and gratitude. But ultimately, we see success as a means to an end, to freedom and flexibility. It seems every time someone reaches the apex, they stop. The architect and the "seminal" building, an artist and his masterpiece, a comedian and his pinnacle, a writer and his greatest achievement. But I gather one's interests ebb and flow, that man must find his way like a river carving out its path over centuries. The river is never satisfied to flow in a straight line, or even consistently over the same path forever. Once accomplished, the course changes, but I'm unsure if the fire simply goes out, or if it just spreads in different directions."

As usual, I had no idea what Noah was talking about. But this time I didn't care. I had more important things to consider. More important thoughts dominated my attention. And anyway, Noah was home now. My part was done.

"My point is," he continued, ignoring every signal I was sending about *my* need to retreat to *my* pointless life. "My point is, if you worry about losing what you have more than enjoying that which you have, then what you have isn't worth a thing."

I stood looking directly into Noah's face, into his eyes. That point resonated with me. That focused my attention. Once again, he had penetrated my very essence. My mind was in chaos, but my heart was open to the unknown.

"And besides," Noah continued, "I'm a devout believer in the philosophy of the late, great Shannon Hoon."

"Oh, yeah," I was on the precipice, ready to be fully emerged in this time with Noah; all I needed now was a slight existential nudge.

"And what exactly is that?"

"'When life is hard, you have to change.'"

That was a direct hit that struck me deeply. I was painfully aware of the unexplainable paradox within me. The fear of losing the life I loved so much made it impossible for me to enjoy this life I loved so much.

With that, we were on the Harley. The monstrous engine thundered below us as I accelerated up the ramp to I-95 South toward New York. The crisp air was biting at my face and slightly stinging my lips, which were now cracking as the smile broadened across my face. And here I thought my adventure was over. Why, it was just getting started.

Chapter 6

Venedocia, Ohio. A very small town in Ohio, Venedocia has been described by its own inhabitants as the "smallest village in Ohio with a homepage." It was a close knit community and an all-American place to live. At its center lived the great Reverend William Binkley, or "Pastor Bill," as everyone in the town referred to him.

A typically middle-aged Clergyman, Pastor Bill was anything but typical. William Binkley hailed from a long lineage of learned, diverse, and accomplished theologians. Born and raised in Pittsburgh, Pennsylvania, he himself went on to receive a Liberal Arts education from Oxford University and even studied for nearly three years at the Vatican's very own seminary school. With no intent to subjugate himself to Catholicism, William Binkley ultimately earned a doctorate in theology from Harvard's Divinity School, and while his Sunday sermons were tailored to his faithful Methodist audience, Pastor Bill could dance elegantly across the broadest volumes of ancient theology, classic literature, and pop culture. Pastor Bill was like no one else in the world. And now he lived in Venedocia, Ohio, by the grace of God, with his wife of eight years and their seven-year-old daughter.

He first met Virginia in Rome. She was visiting with her family at the tender age of eighteen, touring Europe for two weeks during the summer as a reward for being accepted to Harvard back in March. In less than three months, Virginia would begin studies at one of the world's most prestigious universities.

William had been their personal guide one afternoon, giving the family of three a private tour of the Sistine Chapel, St. Peter's Basilica, the Papal Tombs, the Vatican Gardens (he had come to intimately know every inch of them), and the Vatican itself. He did this to satisfy part of his commitment to his large and growing tuition fees, but mostly because he loved the people, their collective history, and his own understanding of a singular power.

Undoubtedly, Virginia was intrigued by his boyish face which was graced with sharp features and gentle angles, topped by his short and graceful blonde hair. His tall, thin frame carried an exuberance she had yet to encounter. Most of all, Virginia was enchanted with his command of history, theology, the Latin language, and the world in general (this one and the next). Virginia had spent only a few short hours in his presence, yet loved him deeply, or at least the concept of him.

When William enrolled at Harvard a year later; destiny smiled elegantly upon the two. On his first day teaching "The History of Ancient Christianity" as a graduate teacher's assistant, William was once again introduced to Virginia, and not entirely by coincidence, Virginia once again found herself in the presence of William's great knowledge.

The couple's relationship and love for one another grew strong over the next several years, and after Virginia graduated, they were married. After completing his doctorate work, the couple moved to Venedocia, where Virginia was born and raised. Within a year, their daughter Lizzie was born.

While their home was a modest three-bedroom bungalow settled on old Main Street near the heart of town, Pastor Bill spent most of his time comforting the congregation he so dearly cared for: the sick, the hurt, the elderly, and the faithful. Only 187 steps from his front door down the tree-lined streets of Venedocia, his Church was a visual symbol of the pillar he, himself, had become in this community.

It was evening, now, just a little past 7:30 as Pastor Bill finished a large glass of sweet iced tea while swaying softly on his front porch rocking chair. It was unusually warm for March, and the song birds were fading with the last of the day's sunshine, replaced by the opening stanza of the tree frog chorus, which started each night right about now. That was his signal. Lizzie would be expecting him, expecting him to tell her a story of grand adventure and surprise. He did this every night, and tonight would be no different. It was never a chore and always a blessing for him to connect with the sweet innocence of his daughter whom he loved so dearly.

Pastor Bill pushed through the screen door, paused briefly to hear the usual creak and slap as it slammed shut behind him, and then skipped every other step as he bounded upstairs toward Lizzie's room. The creek of the old pine floors from the hallway below gave him pause as he reached the halfway point up the wooden staircase.

Gripping the banister with his left hand, he bent over slowly and peered down from the space between the banister and second floor overhang to see Virginia glide to the front door, close it softly, and turn the deadbolt locked. He waited there silently until she turned and looked up at him.

"I love you," she whispered, not so that he could hear, but so that he could see her say those words to him again.

And while he could not hear her words, he knew their meaning and felt them deeply in his heart. He blinked, smiled broadly, and continued toward the top of the stairs.

There were two bedrooms on the second floor. Pastor Bill and Virginia slept in the master bedroom on the first floor, except when Virginia's mother came to visit. Then they would stay in the second floor bedroom, which had been arranged as a guest suite. Pastor Bill and Virginia were usually the only guests that old room saw, with only her mother remaining and in poor health besides.

The other bedroom, directly across the hallway, was Lizzie's. Pastor Bill entered it quietly and found her already in bed, her covers pulled up close to her chin and her eyes already closed.

"Well," he whispered out loud. "I guess she's already asleep, so no story tonight."

Her mouth formed a little smile, then burst into a full giggle.

"Daddy, I'm not really sleeping," she said, her eyes now wide open and full of life. "I was just pretending."

"Well then, in that case ...," Pastor Bill made his way tenderly to her bedside, "I should read you a story about how much I love you. In fact," he produced a small book from behind his back, "I have a book here called 'Guess How Much I Love You,' by Sam McBratney, and the pictures were done by a woman named Anita Jeram."

She smiled broadly as her dad began:

> "'Guess how much I love you ... '
> 'Oh, I don't think I could guess that,' said Big Nutbrown Hare.
> 'This much,' said Little Nutbrown Hare, stretching out his arms as wide as they could go."

After several pages, Pastor Bill would skip forward a couple of pages because he was sure that Lizzie was drifting quickly toward a deep and comfortable sleep, securely fastened beneath her sheets in a bed that rested in a loving home. But he continued,

"" ... I love you as high as I can reach,' said Big Nutbrown Hare.

' ... and I love you all the way down the lane as far as the river,' cried Little Nutbrown Hare."

It wasn't long before Lizzie was fast asleep, and Pastor Bill stopped reading altogether, shut the book, and sat on the edge of Lizzie's bed, studying her angelic face for several minutes longer. After soaking in her radiance, he then rose ever so slowly so as not to disturb his sleeping daughter, turned, and headed for the open door.

"Daddy," she whispered as he reached for the light switch.

Turning his head back toward her gentle voice, his hand remained on the light switch, ready to turn it off for the night, "Hmmm," he said softly, but with slight surprise.

"I love you," her voice again traveled softly across the room.

His heart leaped, and then it sank, and it jumped around in his chest. He loved her so much.

"I love you to the moon and back," he said, parroting the final line from that cute little story he was reading just moments ago.

Lizzie turned over in bed and propped up her curly blond head of hair with her left hand; her deep blue, translucent eyes expressed an endless, imaginative life. Wide awake now, she said back to him, "I love you to God and back."

Caught off guard, Pastor Bill looked down upon the very gift that rooted his life, nourished his soul, and sheltered his heart in times of turmoil. Weeping inside, unfettered outside, yet deeply moved, he flicked the light switch and the room went dark.

"Good night, sweetie."

"What a ridiculous response," he thought in the same instant, "I am more."

"Daddy," the little girl persisted through the dark.

"Yes, Lizzie?" He was now halfway into the hallway.

"Daddy," she repeated, then paused, "what is evil?"

Pastor Bill froze and shivered slightly as the feelings of tenderness and innocence he absorbed from Lizzie turned abruptly to concern combined with a dash of fear. He instinctually moved toward his young daughter, yet the long, silent pause, and accompanying blank stare that followed did nothing to dissuade Lizzie's thirst for an answer. The inquisitive expression on her face demanded it.

"Well, sweetheart," he started slowly, gaining some control over the thrust of anxiety that initially ran unchecked through his emotions, "I don't exactly have a definition for evil."

She listened intently, and her wide eyes glistened with intensity. Pastor Bill had no choice but take this one head on. So, he sauntered slowly back into her room and sat gently at the end of her bed. The only light in the room streamed in from the hallway through the half-open doorway, casting soft shadows. Pastor Bill delicately placed his hand on the soft blankets covering the small shins of his fragile daughter, then even more delicately considered the words he would place in her mind.

"Lizzie ..." he started slowly, feeling his way carefully, as if entering a minefield alone and with no equipment.

"Yes, Daddy?"

"I'm wondering what you are thinking about," he paused shortly and rubbed his chin. "Did you hear about something at school?"

"No," she said, quite sure of her answer. "When Papa died, and Mommy was very sad," she clenched her little blanket a little more tightly, "Mommy said that what made Papa sick was evil and she wished it never existed ... so, I'm kind of scared evil will make you and Mommy sick."

Pastor Bill leaned in and gently kissed his daughter, the fear that clenched him eased as his grasp on the root of the question took hold.

"Oh, Lizzie, Mommy and Daddy will live for a long, long time. You don't have to worry about that."

Those simple words immediately put her at ease. She loosened her grip on the little blanket and lay back further, her blonde, curly hair spread out on the stack of soft pillows. Her face was a great deal more peaceful.

"But our souls can give us a false sense of durability because of their everlasting nature," Bill continued, trying to simplify a complex belief, a certainty in his existence. "The soul is like a big boulder, a really strong concrete foundation. But the body is more like a straw hut built upon it. So it's important we take care of both, eating the right foods and exercising our bodies while fortifying our souls with life's rich nutrients."

Lizzie seemed content, but Bill felt he hadn't quite answered his daughter's question directly, but he also wanted to change the subject so he didn't actually have to answer her question quite so directly.

"And sometimes our bodies get sick, but our souls never do. Our souls live on forever, which means you, me, and Mommy will always be together."

Lizzie was happy, and she was drifting off to sleep, but she did have another question for her Dad as she drifted off for the night.

"So, where does sickness come from?" she whispered her last words of the day.

Pastor Bill smiled down upon her and gently patted her blanket covered legs.

"I don't know where sickness comes from, but I know prayer can heal. And I don't believe that sickness itself is evil, but I also don't know why sickness, or suffering in general, exists naturally in our world. But this I do know," Bill leaned in some for additional effect. "How we choose to face adversity and suffering has great meaning. Only we can be responsible for our thoughts and actions. Suffering can be a constant reminder that life is fragile, that life is wonderful, that life is wonderfully fragile."

Lizzie was not really even paying attention to him, she was now drifting into a deep sleep, but Pastor Bill thought a few more words would finish the job, and they were important for developing his own perspective on the matter.

"Suffering can also be transforming, and can ignite powerful change for the better. Great leaders like Mahatma Gandhi and Martin Luther King have transformed great suffering and injustice into great peace and justice. And when Papa died, even though she was suffering, Mommy was able to better understand that God is with us, and God hurts when we suffer and wants to help ease our pain, to help us through. Our God is with us and within us; it is up to us to let Him into our lives."

Lizzie was now fast asleep. Bill tucked her blankets in around her.

"Don't worry, Lizzie, we'll all be together forever," he whispered with one last great look of love and adoration. And with that, he got up to leave.

Bill was startled momentarily by the shape of his loving wife, leaning on the doorway and looking in with her kind and gentle face.

"Virginia, you scared me to death," he said in a whispered laugh, playfully grabbing at her.

She laughed quietly, and headed quickly down the hall toward the stairs.

"How long were you standing there?" He was now only a step or two behind her as she reached the first floor.

"Oh, long enough, Bill. Long enough."

He followed her into the family room and took a seat in his deep leather chair directly across from Virginia, who sat modestly on the sofa.

"What?" he exclaimed his innocence, reacting to her stare that was in place of a guilty finger pointing at him.

"Bill, she's only seven years old."

"I know," he stirred his finger gently on the rich leather, looking a bit sheepish. "But I want to be sure we build her value system as strong as we can, while we can. Heck, I once read that a child's entire moral system is completely in place by the time they turn eight!"

Virginia was relaxed; she knew her husband well and loved him very much.

"And besides," he continued, "I was talking through that concept to a large degree to better understand my own thinking on the matter."

"Ah-ha. And yet, you never quite answered her question, did you?"

Bill and Virginia had spent many, many hours, seated in these very positions, discussing such topics since they moved into this loving home. They cherished this time and these discussions.

"No, I guess I didn't," Bill adjusted in his chair. "Most likely because I don't quite have the answer properly formed in my own mind."

Bill paused for several moments, gathering his thoughts. Virginia waited patiently without breaking the silence.

"Suffering, I believe," he started again in a methodical, thoughtful way, "happens because you do God's will. That is, doing what's right even when doing what's right is not the popular choice. I also believe suffering happens because you disobey God's will, being driven by virtues like greed, apathy, or ignorance."

Virginia considered this opening position. And while she appreciated its simplicity, she expected a lot more.

"Sure, Bill, I understand and agree. But suffering and evil are not the same thing. And while Lizzie may not have been clear on that point, I certainly am. So, then, Bill, how are they different, and what purpose do they serve in a perfect world created by a perfect God?"

Bill drew in a long and hearty breath. Virginia was no lightweight. She was always a formidable contributor to any discussion. And tonight, she was challenging him to challenge himself. Some of Bill's greatest thinking emerged this way.

"The question of suffering and the obvious extensions related to evil have created many philosophical paradoxes for me throughout my life, particularly related to the nature of good and evil. For example, cancer exists and it creates great suffering for the many touched by its devastating impacts. Did God create cancer? Is cancer good?"

Virginia looked a little perplexed.

"And?"

Pastor Bill paused for what could have been an indefinite amount of time needed to ponder his approach.

"And ... I believe that the words and actions of people can have profound and lasting impact on others."

Her perplexed look turned to total confusion.

"Bill, what in the world does that have to do with the existence of evil?"

"Well," he started again slowly, "When I was a small child— I was only six or seven at the time—I remember asking a burning question in my Sunday school class, one that had been troubling my young mind for some time since first hearing about it in church. As the class ended, we were being shepherded into a neat line waiting for our parents to claim us. And as I passed one of the ladies chaperoning our class that day, someone I had never seen before, I knew that the time for action was at hand."

Virginia sat up and leaned in more closely. His vulnerability penetrated her, and she reacted in kind.

"She didn't notice me at first, but I was persistent, and I eventually got her full attention, and I asked that total stranger the most important question of my life."

Virginia was now vested heavily in her husband's story.

"And what was that question?" she asked with care and sincerity.

"Do you believe in hell?"

Virginia sat back, a little surprised at this change in direction.

"And without hesitation, she said to me, 'No, dear. I don't.' And when I asked why not, her simple wisdom blew over me like a gentle breeze. She said merely, 'Because I believe that God is the Creator of all things, and that all things God creates are good. And I don't believe God created hell. So, I don't believe it exists.' And in an instant, that simple logic from a total stranger had shaped my belief system in a profound and lasting way. Delivered by a woman, a person, a stranger

I can remember only in the slightest way. A nameless, faceless stranger from my past helped form the foundation of a moral system that persists today."

"So," Virginia persisted, "you don't believe suffering, or evil, even exist?"

Bill laughed in a polite, but contradictory way.

"No, they exist alright. But I don't believe God created either."

Bill paused. Virginia's intense stare reinforced his need to go on.

"Suffering starts when those you love most, or you yourself, experience pain, injustice, or some other harm inflicted by another. Sometimes suffering is a natural part of the world we live in, inflicted by disease or chance. And in both of these cases, to explain this injustice, I often hear that 'It's God's will.' And yet, it's impossible for me to believe that God *wills* suffering." Bill paused to let his words soak in. "Why do we insist on putting God in the middle of every action and outcome, where even the most diminutive detail has been prearranged? That's preposterous! We are here together, living with freewill. And that means we are active participants in a dynamic life. I mean, what would be the point of prayer, faith, and life itself if every choice and outcome was already predestined? That seems more like an excuse to avoid making the right decisions, to not fight the battles that need to be fought, to not live life they way God wants us to live it. We have an acute responsibility and an urgency to actively shape the outcome, to participate in this life, to advance each other, our neighbors, humanity at large, toward a closer reflection of God. 'It's God's will,' that's like storing our child away in her room for her entire life so she would be safe from the cruelties of our world but live a miserable and pointless existence, powerless to experience the beauty and grandeur of this miraculous world God created, unable to experience it with others who are just as amazed by its perfection. Any parent making this choice would be a monster."

"Yes, Bill. I see your point now. Suffering, while certainly terrible, is a natural byproduct of the design, where freewill is a foundational pillar." Virginia looked for some assurance she had kept up with his thoughts. "But then, doesn't that mean the original design included the possibility of pain and suffering, based on the infinite choices we have made throughout time?"

Bill thought about this for several moments.

"I suppose that is possible. It's also possible that pain and suffering, or more specifically how we respond to those extraordinary challenging parts of our lives, are necessary in our progression toward a closer reflection of God. And yet God does everything he can to reduce our suffering without violating our freewill."

Virginia was delighted, but not quite fully content.

"And evil?"

"Ah, yes, evil," Bill scratched his chin as he always did when he already had his answer. "Unlike love, beauty, kindness, and all things good, evil does not inherently reside in each of us just waiting to be unleashed. No. Evil is more like a desert cactus, a plant that takes years to reach maturity but becomes a robust life force. It doesn't need much to establish itself, it's highly adaptive, and it can thrive in the most desolate environments for hundreds of years. Often, evil's seed is the individual's selfish desire, that which can be fertilized by others' discontent, and it grows feverishly through hardening hearts, then blooms when the boundaries of our own desires find no end. And once mature, it can thrive unchallenged for centuries. Evil is rooted in a person's ability to rationalize actions that cause pain and suffering to others—physically, emotionally, or spiritually. Eventually, this rationalization enables one to separate from God's love, and this, Virginia, is where true evil exists, where the choice to love and be loved no longer exists."

"So, did God create evil?"

"No. Quite the contrary. God has provided each and every one of us everything we need, including the *responsibility* to prevent evil, to stamp out its very existence, so the collective good can be a closer reflection of Him. It's just up to each of us to do our part."

And with that, Virginia stood up, walked gracefully over to Bill, and draped herself around him with a pure heart, with a pure love.

"I love you so much, William Binkley," she said, squeezing him tighter. "This family is so blessed, and I couldn't be happier."

They stayed in each other's arms for several more minutes, soaking in the goodness that was life, goodness that was their life.

"It's late," Bill finally broke the silence, "let's get to bed."

And yet, as Bill and Virginia Binkley slept peacefully, securely fastened beneath their sheets, in their bed that rested in their loving home, evil persisted.

Suddenly, out of the darkness came the loudest, most obtrusive silence never heard. It was a violent crack in time and space lasting only a few seconds, shattered when the back door was violently kicked in by a band of men dressed in black hooded sweatshirts, masks covering their twisted faces, insolence covering their black hearts.

Bill and Virginia were trapped, locked inside their room and unable to do anything but scream and claw at the door that kept them from protecting that which mattered most to them individually and together. Lizzie was their world. Lizzie was their very essence.

"Quiet her down, stop her from squirming."

Bill and Virginia's pain intensified knowing their little girl needed them now more than ever, and there was not a thing they could do to help.

"Hurry," another voice in the hallway rasped.

"It's done, Maven, let's go."

Bill and Virginia's blood ran cold as they heard the dilapidated truck outside roar off into the darkness. Absolute silence followed.

Then suddenly, their bedroom door flung open, releasing them like wild animals into the hallway. Bill burst through the back door, but like a mist evaporating in the morning sun, the kidnappers had vanished into the night with Lizzie. They were gone, and so was she. But the pain that was ignited would burn out of control, and it had plenty of fuel to burn down his soul. Pastor Bill had his definition now. Evil and suffering were no longer concepts to be debated among scholars. They were alive in his life and stabbed cruelly and mercilessly at his heart. Worse, their torment ignited a lust for vengeance that would burn feverishly in the nights to come.

Chapter 7

A nna was tired, fueled only by stimulating thought and discussion. Sixteen hours in the car had left her exuberant body and soul in tangles, unaccustomed to the constant confinement and monotony of a long interstate road trip. Anna was ready for a break.

"Halfway there," she thought in a veiled attempt to motivate her mind to fight what she knew was a losing battle. Anna wanted to stop and stretch her legs. Anna wanted to stop and stretch her mind. She was ready to explode, a ticking time bomb in a place she didn't know, suspended in time from sitting idle for too long.

"Mind if we stop?" she finally quipped at Noah, who remained unchanged, slouched in the passenger-side seat with his hat pulled down over his face for the past several hours.

"Not a bit," came the reply. "I was thinking the very same thing."

"Are you hungry?" Anna asked in hopes of getting some guidance from Noah on a decision she had already made.

"Not especially. Anywhere is fine with me," Noah responded and patted her hand gently without moving at all and without looking up from beneath his hat.

And so they rolled on down the highway. Anna was being silently tormented by the passing of white stripes and the constant "clump, bump" of the sectioned highway. Noah slept, but still she pushed on. She pushed on toward something, anything, looking for a sign—any sign—that might signal that a cold drink and shade tree were up ahead— anything that might comfort her in her time of great discomfort. But it never came. Not for some time, at least.

"Noah," she spoke softly, almost existentially, as if she were not even speaking at all, or maybe hoping not to be heard.

Noah paused intentionally before responding, shifting his body so as to face her more directly and removing that old, ragged hat to reveal his huge and wanting eyes that now searched Anna up and down for deeper meaning.

"What is it, Anna?"

Anna stared forward, watching the road come, then slip past and disappear in the rearview mirror behind them. Her grip on the wheel tightened slightly. She knew that Noah already knew something was bothering her, and that made her even more nervous.

"What's on your mind?" Noah prompted her again.

"Noah?"

"Yes, Anna?"

"Are we doing the right thing?"

The question hung in the cabin of that compact Jetta, muted only slightly by the humming of its ill-tuned engine and the slightly off-balance tires driving enormous friction against the asphalt below.

"Do you feel we're doing the right thing, Anna?" Noah started in his deliberate manner. "More importantly, do you feel like *you're* doing the right thing, Anna?"

She thought for some time about Noah's point and then about the words she would use to respond to him.

"I know being here with you is good, Noah," she finally responded.

He smiled without her knowing.

"And I know that helping you is the right thing," she continued, "that your mother needs you," Anna's body language corrected what she knew Noah wanted to hear.

"She needs us."

They sat quietly, resting peacefully in their stationary chairs as the miles hurled violently around them.

"But," Anna once again broke the calmly disturbing sounds of the highway's monotonous melody. " … but I'm scared to tell you the truth." Anna paused and collected her thoughts.

Noah listened patiently.

"I'm not scared of you, of course," Anna reassured herself. "No, nothing like that."

"Well, what then, Anna? What are *you* scared of?"

"To be honest … the future. *My* future. I mean, I've walked away from my fifth job in as many years. This adventure will eventually end, and I will ultimately be left with what I started." Anna slammed the steering wheel in an awkwardly feminine way, but Noah recognized it to be pure passion.

"And what is that, Anna?" Noah already knew, but he asked anyway.

"My life, Noah. My life!"

Anna was emotional, but she was not anywhere near crying. Anna rarely shed a tear. But she felt deeply, and this particular subject cut to her core. The thought—or threat—of reuniting with her parents terrified her.

"Well, Anna," Noah responded thoughtfully, soulfully, "you are clearly an amazing person, and doing the right thing in this world is rare indeed."

Anna smiled. She even relaxed a bit.

"But know this," Noah's voice darkened, "the world is being murdered by apathy, and only the engaged can help it."

Anna tried to understand, but there was very little time before he spoke his next words.

"There's a place," he said, pointing to the green exit sign containing a simple Exxon logo. "It doesn't look like much, but I guarantee we'll find a cool drink, a place to rest, and the warm embrace of two friends who may have forgotten what a good hug feels like."

Anna's fears slowly evaporated. She glanced briefly in Noah's direction and smiled abruptly. There was something very special about Noah, and that she knew for sure. Helping him was the right thing for her to do, and for now, she knew it was the *only* thing for her to do.

Another mile down the road, Anna pulled onto the exit ramp, coming to a complete stop at the end of the road. There really wasn't much of a decision from there. To the right, Anna spotted the old Exxon station situated in a field of nothing. There were two pumps in front of a little store that she hoped at least sold cold soda. To the left, there was absolutely nothing, unless an endless road cutting through an endless desert was something.

Anna pulled the little Jetta up to the first pump.

"You go on inside," Noah said, "I'll pump us some gas."

Anna smiled. She appreciated that small gesture. She typically recognized all the small gifts she received from those around her, so she popped open her door and stood upright into the warm Texas afternoon. Anna looked around purposefully, then drew in a strong, dusty breath as she strode confidently toward the store. And while her observational prowess had been dulled slightly by the highway lackluster, Anna did notice an old, wooden picnic table resting about twenty yards to the right of the old cinder block store, and just beyond that, another twenty or thirty yards or so, there was a small, brick ranch home. Anna could not decide which was stranger: the fact that she had not noticed the little house before, or the fact that she dismissed its presence in her search for a cold drink and a bite to eat.

And as Anna had all but ignored this setting, she was stopped by the sudden impact of what she saw. There was also an old, rusted swing set, and a small child, a young girl, swung aimlessly on its only curved, black swing seat. The old chains made a faint and methodical screech as she floated back and forth, back and forth. Anna squinted for a better look. She could not make out the little girl's face, but watched her swing slowly in that dirty lot. Not too high. Not too low. The little girl just gently swung to and fro, staring straight ahead into a future that had no future. Anna wanted to imagine she did not exist. She was like a pink fish waiting for someone, anyone. And the reality of that little girl's desolation on that lonely swing was almost too much for her to bear.

Eventually shaking off the scene that had rendered her frozen, Anna pushed through the old screen door of the store. She paused briefly just inside to take in her surroundings and to get a bearing on where she needed to go. The store was brightly lit, partially with the sun streaming in from the dusty windows, and partially from the large fluorescent lights that quietly hummed overhead. It smelled musty, though, like the concrete floors had molded in areas where moisture gathered and stagnated. Two rows of wooden shelves housed various snack foods, candies, and other convenience store goods. Anna was sure the shelves were handmade, thrown together quickly with cheap plywood and coated carelessly with a thick layer of white paint. Surprisingly, the little store had an old-fashioned diner set up at the far end.

Anna moved cautiously toward the counter that stretched across the back of the store. Eight red stools rested in front of the old, linoleum counter top. Each had obviously seen a lot of use over the years as their stitches had become undone and their red leather was faded, worn, and cracked. A tall, wiry man that looked to be in his sixties stood behind the counter. His strong, wrinkled old hands were placed flatly on the middle of the counter, and he was leaning over, talking quietly to several portly gentlemen occupying three red stools at the far end of the counter. The stools embraced their occupants like dear old friends but seemed to whine slightly at the load they were forced to bear.

Anna quickly sized them all up. Each man was wearing jeans or overalls and wearing a button-down work shirt with the sleeves rolled up to the elbows. One of the men wore an old Dr. Pepper baseball cap, and another wore a wide-brimmed straw hat. They clearly spent time together in the same barber shop, sporting short cuts that bordered on crew cuts. As Anna studied them, the four men stopped talking all at once and craned their necks, as if choreographed to do so in unison, in order to take in the strange woman that had entered their domain.

"Afternoon," came the thick Texas drawl from the man behind the counter. "Can I help ya?"

Anna gathered herself. She glanced quickly through the dirt-stained window for some additional confidence that Noah was still with her. The wiry man followed her line of sight to take in Noah out at the pump, but the other men never took their eyes off Anna.

"Can I help ya find anything, young lady?" he tried again, this time moving out from behind the counter and sauntering slowly, cautiously toward Anna.

"I ... we ... we're looking for a little something to eat," Anna stammered a bit, then regained her composure. "And something cold to drink," she said with great confidence. "We sure could use something refreshing to drink."

"Well in that case, come right over here."

The old man's face brightened a bit, which relaxed Anna some, but she remained on edge. The men on their stools went back to their plates that were full of home cooking.

"The wife made a fresh batch of peach iced tea just about an hour ago, and I would be happy to make up a couple of fresh sandwiches for ya. What'll ya have?"

Anna moved toward the far end of the counter. She was tempted to curl up in one of the worn stools but remained standing.

"Have you got any turkey?"

The man smiled, "How about a couple of fresh turkey sandwiches, with some Swiss cheese, sprouts, and some delicious homemade chutney spread?"

Anna's spirits soared.

"That sounds perfect."

Anna relaxed even more. She even felt a little guilty being so suspicious of these nice old men.

And with that, the man busied himself with the sandwich making. And as he did so, an awkward silence hung over the group. Not a word emerged from the men at the end of the bar. And while Anna was more relaxed now, she stayed focused on the old man, once in awhile glancing out the dirty window at Noah, who had finished pumping gas and was now loitering around the car.

"Where ya headed?" The old man stayed busy, seemingly rushing to put the meal together.

"Louisiana," Anna answered.

Noticing the license plates on her car, he quipped, "That's a long way from California," the old man coupled his statement with a glance implying something, but what, Anna did not know.

"I've got family there. I'm headed home."

"Well, then, home is a wonderful place to be headed," he said, gently shoving the wrapped sandwiches into a white paper bag. "It's even better when you get there. Can I get you anything else?" he asked, pushing the bag of sandwiches and the iced teas toward her somewhat abruptly.

"No. Thank you, this is just fine."

The man stood over her, feigning patience as she fished around in her purse for the $32.55 she needed to pay for the gas, sandwiches, and cold iced teas.

"Thank ya kindly," he said as Anna finished laying the bills and coins out onto the counter. "Hope your trip home works out like you want it to." His words were kind, but Anna did not find them sincere. And as she turned to leave, Anna paused and turned back to the man with a question on her face.

"Did ya forget something, young lady?"

"No," Anna started slowly, and with great deliberation, "but I was wondering if you knew who that little girl was outside on the swing set."

Suddenly, instinctually, the old man shot a quick, serious look at the three others sitting at the opposite end of the counter. Trying to cover up his obvious and odd reaction, the old man brightened uncharacteristically.

"Sure, I do: that's my granddaughter. She's visitin' with us while her parents are off to some damn place."

Anna immediately went into a high state of alert. Careful not to give her state of concern away, she mustered a friendly smile as the old man stared back at her. One of the three men, the one sitting in the middle, slowly turned and looked at Anna, too.

"Well, thanks again for the sandwiches," she said lifting the bag in their direction, then quickly made her way out of the store and into the dry, Texas air.

Anna took a half dozen steps toward Noah, who was now back in the little black Jetta with his hat once again pulled down over his face. But a greater force stopped her in the moment. Glancing once again in the direction of the swing set, Anna followed her heart and changed her course entirely. And within the next minute, she found herself sitting at the worn picnic table just feet from the young girl who continued to drift aimlessly on the old, rusty swing set, back and forth, back and forth.

The little girl barely even noticed her as Anna removed her sandwich from the bag and unwrapped it on the old table top. Anna looked nervously from the store where the men were watching, to the Jetta where Noah slept, and back to the swing set where the little girl remained.

"Hello," Anna said eventually, then calmly took a bite of her sandwich.

After an instant, the sweet little girl turned her attention to Anna, like she was suddenly awakened from a deep trance. She continued to swing slowly back and forth, back and forth, but the life reentered her face and filled her eyes with hope, as if she were waiting for this moment all of eternity.

"Hello," she responded in the sweetest, most innocent voice. "What's your name?"

"My name is Anna," she answered back with a caring smile. "What's yours?"

"Lizzie."

"Lizzie. That sure is a pretty name." An awkward silence followed, and Anna looked for the right words to keep the conversation going.

"That swing sure looks fun," Anna continued the hard work of cultivating a discussion with this little soul.

"I guess so."

"Is that your favorite thing to do?" Anna continued to eat her lunch in a feeble attempt to ease the suspicion she perceived was radiating from within the store.

"Not really," the little girl continued, but then happily exclaimed, "my favorite thing to do is play with my dollies. I have lots of them, you know." The little girl's mood once again turned somber. "But ..."

"But what?" Anna prompted her to go on.

"Well, they're not here with me, so I can't play with them," she said, her little eyes stared back to the ground.

"That's too bad," Anna continued delicately. "When I was your age, I had lots of dollies, too."

"You did?" The happiness and excitement returned.

"Sure, I did, and I would dress them up and comb their hair and do all sorts of fun things with them."

"That's what I do!" The small child was quite excited now, and after listening to the little girl chatter on and on about her dolls and the games she would play with them, Anna sought her answer.

"Does your grandpa not have dolls for you to play with?"

The girl stopped swinging. She looked at Anna with a confused look on her face. Not that the little girl was confused about the question, but more like she was confused that Anna was confused. And then her words pierced Anna like nothing else had up to that moment in her life.

"That's not my grandpa. You know I don't belong here."

Anna was instantly overwhelmed with emotion. Fear, courage, love, and hate all simultaneously surged within her. Her mind demanded that she walk away, as she usually did from the real issues confronting her life. But her heart commanded her to stop and think, to do the right thing. Her mind was stronger.

Anna quickly crumpled up the remainder of her sandwich and shoved it back into the bag. She stood up abruptly, trying not to raise any more attention from within the store, but walked briskly toward Noah, who was now observing her actions with great intensity.

"Don't go," Anna heard the little voice behind her say.

Then Anna noticed at least two faces staring out from within the store, which focused her more intently on making it to the little black Jetta. Fifty-two quick steps carried Anna from the helpless, destitute little girl to her own safety within the familiar confines of the Jetta. Once inside, she inserted the key into the ignition, and the trusty old Jetta came to life immediately. Anna paused, waiting for some guidance, anything from her wise, old friend of two days. Nothing.

"Noah?" she turned to him looking for answers. Her eyes told the story, her mouth couldn't say the words. The conflict, fear, passion, and empathy consumed her.

Still, Noah sat silent. His eyes refused to meet hers and remained on the little girl who seemed destined to swing her life away on that dusty highway.

Anna dropped the transmission into drive, and the old Jetta responded by lurching forward slightly.

"Anna," Noah said firmly, but in a coaxing, patriarchal way. "Martin Luther King, Jr. once said, 'Cowardice asks the question, 'Is it safe?' Expediency asks the question, 'Is it politic?' Vanity asks the question, 'Is it popular?' But, conscience asks the question, 'Is it right?' And there comes a time when one must take a position that is neither safe, nor politic, nor popular, but one must take it because one's conscience tells one that it is right.' It's time for you to put those words to work."

Anna squeezed the steering wheel tighter, then ignored Noah's advice by slowly moving her foot off the brake causing the Jetta to roll forward.

"Anna," Noah said again. This time there was more urgency in his voice, and his left hand gently grabbed her right arm.

Anna ignored the stars, the sun, and the moon as she stomped on the gas and accelerated that little Jetta toward the highway. They would certainly pass right by the little girl on their way out of that forgotten station and away from her forever. Anna made every effort to avoid looking in her direction at all. Approaching on the left, Anna thoughtlessly shifted her gaze toward Lizzie, who continued to swing mindlessly on that old rusted swing set, hopelessly drifting in a dazed existence she did not understand.

The brakes wrenched and the wheels smoked as the brave little Jetta responded to Anna's foot commands. The little girl looked curiously in the direction of all the commotion, noticing only that the back door of the Jetta had mysteriously flipped open. Like no other moment in her life, Anna wasn't actually thinking about herself; her thoughts were only on saving that little girl.

"Get in," Anna said rather softly for the moment, but connecting directly with Lizzie and her blank, surprised stare.

The little girl instantly stopped swinging and looked curiously at Anna and Noah, as if asking permission for her dream to become a reality.

"Get in," Anna said again, this time even more softly, but her words rang out across that dusty property like a church bell.

The little girl smiled broadly, something Anna had not expected, and then she confidently hopped from the swing, and without once looking back, made herself a part of their lives.

When she heard the back door slam shut, Anna once again stomped on the gas, squealing the tires and spinning the old Jetta out onto the highway and down the onramp toward the freeway. They rode frozen in time for several miles, not a sound, absolute silence, The minutes turned into miles and the miles turned into an hour. Anna's eyes incessantly darted from the road in front of them to the rearview mirror, expecting to see Lizzie's grandfather—or whoever that was— and his friends, giving chase, or maybe the police. Or at least tears in Lizzie's eyes as they increased the distance from where she was and where she was going. But the little girl sat angelically in the back seat with nothing but a sweet smile on her face.

"God, what am I doing?!" Anna's voice exploded in the silence.

"You did the right thing," Noah replied. His voice, his words were confident, but they didn't make Anna feel any better.

"The right thing?!" Anna was now erratic. "I've stolen a little girl!"

Anna was breathing hard now. She was clearly panicking, and the situation had become too much for her to handle.

"We've got to take her back."

The logic had returned to her thoughts, but her emotions continued to control her actions.

"No, Anna, we can't do that, and you know it," Noah remained steadfast.

"We have to take her somewhere, somewhere safe, somewhere she will be taken care of," Anna was clearly exasperated. "I can't do this!"

"She will be taken care of right here, with us." And while his tone was reassuring, Anna did not accept his words.

"No! No, Noah. This is crazy … and most likely totally illegal!"

"Yes, but we both know it's right."

"How do we know it's right, Noah? How do I know I haven't done something terribly wrong?"

And then suddenly, unexpectedly, a calm and gentle breeze blew in from behind, calming the storm in front. Anna's conflict and anxiety were intercepted with a magical, powerful sensibility. A small voice from the back seat braced the foundations of years to come.

"You've saved me, and you've quite possibly saved us all from a certain, miserable end."

Chapter 8

It was just about dark as Noah and I rolled off Interstate 81 deep in southern Virginia. We had been riding that Harley hard for over eight hours—through New York City, across the northern suburbs of New Jersey, down the picturesque mountains of Pennsylvania, and deep into Virginia. The eight hours passed in a matter of minutes as the sun, the wind, and the sublime scenery around us blew away our thoughts and kept us perfectly in sync with the living moment.

And while my mind was willing, my body had been pushed too far. My legs were numb and my hands and fingers tingled from gripping the vibrating handlebars, but it was my back that hurt the most. Down low, near my tailbone, the sitting and bumping for such a long and arduous time had taken its toll. I was tired and needed to rest.

Without any real plan, I continued a mile or two down that old rural road. Up ahead, I noticed an old barn, offset in a field about a quarter mile away. The large but faded American flag painted on the worn out roof was what caught my eye. There was a little dirt road, really more of a dirt path, leading up to the barn through the overgrown prairie grass. I maneuvered the Harley gently toward our home for the night.

Coming to a rest in front of the dilapidated structure, I cut the engine off, and we were met with silence. A slight ringing in my ear remained momentarily, but that was soon replaced with the peaceful harmony of rural southern Virginia nightlife. The frogs and crickets, in perfect harmony with the other nocturnal animals, were coming to life for the night.

Noah and I eased our aching frames off the bike and stared at the old barn for a minute or two. Clearly, no one had used it for quite some time. There were several holes in the roof, much of the wood was splintered or rotting, and the old cinder block foundation had shifted in the soft soil, causing the entire building to lean awkwardly to the right. But it was good enough for me and Noah.

We stepped inside. It was dusk, now, and harder to see inside the confines of the barn. Thankfully, there was not much to see. There were four stables, two on each side, and a small loft, without a ladder to reach it, in the back. I busied myself poking through each of the stables, finding a couple of old wool horse blankets crumpled up in the corner of one. I shook out the dirt and bugs, then carried my find back to the center of the barn where I found Noah standing over a stack of dry tinder and a few small logs he had just gathered.

"One thing you learn living outdoors, you gotta have a fire," he said, kneeling before his wood and neatly arranging the kindling in a box shape over a pile of dry tinder.

Within minutes, we had a nice, warm, small fire burning. It was amazing how uplifting that simple beacon was. Illuminating the inside of the barn and warming the cool Virginia air around us, it made the barn almost hospitable.

Quietly, and with focus, we arranged our horse blankets on either side of the fire. I lay down on the bottom half, which helped soften the dirt floor, then folded the top half over the top of me, which made me feel slightly more protected from the Virginia night critters.

Lying on my side, I folded my arm awkwardly to support my head and stared deeply into the burning embers of our little fire. The frogs and crickets and birds and raccoon chatter intermingled with the quiet popping of the fire. My body ached and my eyes were heavy, but then suddenly, and without warning, I became overwhelmed lying on the floor of that barn wrapped in a dirty old blanket next to a dirty man.

"Noah?" That was the first word I had spoken since we stopped. In fact, that was the first word I had spoken in hours.

"Yes?" Came the familiar voice full of confidence, full of assurance.

"I'm a little scared."

Noah let the words hang between us for a moment before responding, then let out his opening position. "Of course, you're scared. I'm scared. We're all scared."

Noah propped himself up on his elbow to get a better look at me. I did the same, so I could get a better look at him.

"I don't care whether you're running a Fortune 500 company or playing in a garage band down the street. I don't care who you are. Fear, concern, doubt, pain—we all experience those powerful feelings. It's how we respond to them and use them for good, to do the right thing: that's what defines us as people."

Once again, Noah spoke words that I did not fully understand, and the confused look on my face prompted him to go on.

"Life hates to give you any constructive feedback," Noah continued. "And you won't find it here. Well, maybe you'll find a little. But who really cares? You are the one that's in control."

Noah paused for emphasis. His deep, intense eyes grabbed me. Noah wanted to be sure he had my full attention.

"It starts with you. But it's about everyone else," Noah said, and stirred the fire a bit before continuing. "Let me explain what I mean. You see, too many of us are driven by a social consciousness that distracts us from following the path we were meant to follow in this life. More importantly, we see the path as a means to the end and not as the fundamental purpose."

Noah waited, as he often did, to let me digest his thoughts.

"Answers," Noah continued, "are found on the path and during the journey. It is this interpersonal reflection that should drive our thoughts, our actions, and our place in the world among people, so take peace in your path."

My look said it all.

"You disagree?"

"That's a nice thought," I started with a scoff, "but there are far too many powerful ideologies in the world that drive the collective behavior. What you think, and how you act, are predominantly influenced by your exposure to authoritative institutions such as religion, government, and economies. These powerful superstructures create undeniable constructs such as laws, money, social acceptance, and so on. The average person doesn't stand a chance at overcoming these prepackaged ways of living life with his or her own critical thoughts and introspection. Even if they could, there is certainly no real outlet available to the individual in which to change or shape the prevailing ideology on any meaningful level. "

Noah looked disappointed in my cynical, academic response. Noah often looked disappointed when I tried to spar intellectually at his level.

"I have witnessed many people," Noah started again, "accept the social consciousness as too powerful for them to be anything but mediocre, and the inertia of ideology keeps them from being great and doing the right thing."

Noah paused and scratched his scraggly beard.

"And more concerning is that much of the perspective on ideology as a concept teaches Marxist theory as its origin, as its purpose, and primary impact on society. In fact, I find that ideologies function and serve the public very differently than creating some false consciousness when influencing the everyday life of people, our social order, and our daily conscientiousness. It's not some authoritative claim to power put forward by a governing elite. While an ideology can build into a forceful wave of influence, it is actually nothing more than how we construct and represent a social reality as it is, or more accurately, how we think it should be. And this starts with individual people: people like you, people like me. People. One at a time; there is no other way."

Noah tossed a small stick on the fire before continuing. "You can choose how to influence the tide at any given time, for good or for bad, but as people, we inherently know one is better than the other. And we inherently know we are more, but we so seldom choose to be more. To declare, as Marx did, that ideology is a false consciousness seems out of touch with the practices of real people in real life, overlooking the real, day to day exposure of human behavior to an ideology and vice versa."

Noah shifted his position again, laying flat on his back and speaking up into the open, starry sky we could see in between the cracks and holes in the old barn's roof.

"A lived ideology of everyday life," Noah continued, "is not some misconstrued sense of the word in politics, academics, or professional thinkers. In this sense, ideology is nothing more than an explanation, or a justification, of behavior created in and by a person or group of people to better understand and interpret our reality. And *you* have the ability to influence both," Noah emphasized by pointing his long, dirty finger directly at me without looking in my direction. "*You* should promote critical thinking within your own mind and within the minds around you. The influence *you* wield is mighty because an ideology cannot exist without people to accept it."

Noah paused, a long dramatic pause to punctuate his final point, the real point he wanted me to understand.

"Evil cannot exist without a single person embracing it as a concept. Drop it from your life, and it ultimately disappears from the world."

I was confused. "So, is ideology good, or is ideology bad?"

Noah jumped on the opportunity to respond to such a ridiculous question.

"Ideology is such a ridiculous phenomenon. Humans," he paused, throwing the last of the small sticks onto the dying fire. "humans create a social sense of order, constructing theories in order to provide a framework for how to deal with issues of controversy and dissonance, or frankly, how to behave in everyday situations. We lean on ideology to organize tremendous complexities in our world, and ideology works in a circular momentum, shaping reality, smoothing the edges of uneasiness for us. Reality does not exist without language, without words. When we put words together, we shape action, and action is our reality. The danger, simply, is that prepackaged thinking becomes a crutch, ultimately trapping or replacing altogether individual critical thought. Individuals should empower themselves to make inherently rational decisions. 'I gotta get mine' doesn't get a person anywhere. I know that to be true, from personal experience, that is. And it didn't seem to be sending you in the right direction, either."

My mind was heavy with thoughts. My body was heavy with fatigue, but I was energized by Noah's words.

"So," I responded with a slight yawn in my voice, and a large stretch of my arms, "we can actually *create* good?"

Noah smiled broadly. He always smiled broadly when I was on the right track.

"Yes, we can. One's commitment to a set of beliefs is the very basis of how a person defines reality. Reality, you see, only exists through a social consciousness that can be accepted or rejected by any group of people. Of course, we struggle together, putting forth different and conflicting belief systems that vie for a higher position in the social structure. But what if we all accepted harmony as a starting point? Boy, now that would be powerful."

Noah pulled the blanket tightly around him. The late night Virginia air was getting colder around us, but our small fire and burning discussion kept us warm.

"Ironically," Noah continued, "that ability, that simplicity, is right in front of you, in front of us, within our grasp, totally within our control. The challenge is to get others to actively participate in creating or embracing ideologies that are inherently good in nature, to get them to empower themselves in constructing the world as it is, or how it should be: how *we* should be."

Noah took in a long breath before heading down the home stretch.

"It's like music. We all enjoy music; who doesn't enjoy music as an expression? We simply prefer different types, but inherently, the expression is good. So, just because people hold different beliefs does not mean that the beliefs are about different things. In all my years, I've come to understand an absolute truth. We all enjoy peace and kindness and love. And that starts with you. And that starts with me. That starts with each of us, individually."

I shut my eyes but continued to listen to Noah in a dreamlike state. The hours on the road and the heavy conversation were taking their toll. I held on to consciousness with all my might, but I was losing my grip for sure. Noah's words continued but were lost for me in the background of the crackling fire and tree frog songs.

"The fact is, my life started slowly. Everybody's does. No discipline, no morals, no sanctimonious bull shit—just life. My environment corrupted my mind the minute I was born. Too bad, because before you start living, you start experiencing, especially that which gave you life. And only after you've lived do you start experiencing it again. Life is not breathing. Fish breathe. Life is bigger. Life is much bigger. And life is connected. The only way to be successful is to make those around you successful. Instead of killing a man and taking his wallet, make him successful and enjoy a lifelong sense of fulfillment and prosperity. Stop being pathetic. It's so easy. An ideology is not meant for an individual. We are nothing without each other. Our lives are meaningless without the context of those we serve. That's our purpose."

Noah looked at me, watched me peacefully drift off to sleep on that dirt floor. He knew this day was done and let out an enormous, cleansing sigh. He knew tomorrow would bring extraordinary events, an inflexion point, a turning point.

"But the fact is," he whispered, closing his own eyes for the night, "living life does start with you. Self-importance, there is nothing without you, connecting with those around you." And with that, Noah fell fast asleep.

That night, I dreamed about a red cat looking at the moon, staring in wonder, staring in awe. I was at peace. Good things happened today, and I couldn't wait to find out what tomorrow would bring. Good things happened today! And as I slept in that old barn, surrounded by that cool Virginia night, Noah's words continued. At least I thought they were Noah's words, but the voice did not sound at all like Noah. I must have been dreaming, but I didn't care. The words were comforting, a part of me, my new reality.

"All the keys we need to open our minds can be found in our own hearts. And those doors we open, they are other people. Sometimes the rooms are empty; sometimes they are full of wonder. But opening the doors is what's important. Good things can happen every day if you want them to, if you make them happen; it's up to you. There is greatness all around you, everywhere you look, everywhere you are, in everything you do, because goodness is in you. Good has always been close to you. It's in your heart; you just need to let it in, or more precisely, let it out. Good is there; it's you that has to make the effort to let it out."

Chapter 9

Pastor Bill, or whoever he was becoming, was ready to exact a justified revenge on the men that had scraped his life from the bottom of their shoes. He knew the probability of finding the men that took his Lizzie was very low, and the likelihood of finding Lizzie herself was even lower. Thankfully for the world, hope was not totally lost ... not yet. Even so, Pastor Bill figured there was plenty of evil in the world to stamp out, and he was not interested in discerning one evil from another. He possessed an insatiable thirst for vengeance, and he was ready to fill his emptiness, the bottomless pit of sadness and anger he had become, with pain, agony, and death. That was the future Pastor Bill chose to create.

Virginia had been immobilized by her own grief. Initially, she had pleaded with Bill to rely on their faith, hope, and prayer. But when Bill refused, his anger blinding him, Virginia retreated within herself. Cutting off the outside world, she fell deeper into despair. Even her own mother couldn't console her; the pain was too much and had overpowered her will. Only one thing would fill her bottomless pit of sadness and anger, and that was having Lizzie back in her arms.

Bill didn't attend to any of Virginia's needs at this point. He was too focused on satisfying his own. Like a storm gathering before unleashing its wrath, Bill left her alone and calmly drove the 200 miles from his sweet town of Venedocia, Ohio to Cleveland. He originally thought about Columbus. It was an hour closer to him, but with a larger population and a very high violent crime rate, Cleveland figured to have plenty of deserving candidates.

He took up residence in an old, rundown motel located in East Cleveland, prepaying for the week. The manager, who seemed to be dying from emphysema, coughed violently as he tossed the keys to room 202 on the counter. He thought it odd that his new tenant prepaid a whole week in advance but was thankful for it. Most of his guests paid by the hour.

As Bill climbed the stairs to his second floor room, he couldn't help but notice the acrid smell of rot. Rotten dreams and aspirations were strewn, spilled, or secreted throughout the staircase. He paused momentarily at the door leading to the second floor rooms, looking upwards toward a moan haunting the breezeway above. This only further hardened his heart.

Room 202 was the first door on his right. The hallway was dimly lit and dank from a leaky roof or pipe. Bill gave it no notice as he inserted the old key into the rusty lock, then turned it to open a door down a path that could destroy him and the world as he knew it, or hoped it to be.

Once inside, Bill surveyed the Spartan room. A single bed was shoved up against the wall to his left, an old bureau against the wall to his right, and by the small window rested a folding chair. The old, shag carpet was worn and stained. It smelled like hopelessness.

Bill tossed the duffel bag down onto the bed; it made a clanging noise as the metal weapons jolted, shifted, and then settled again. Bill found his way to the folding chair, pulling it close to the window. He pulled the thick curtain back just enough to peer down to the street below. It was dusk, now, and the local pests were streaming out of every hole in the area, looking to satisfy their hunger with any unsuspecting meal they came upon.

As Bill stared down upon them, his mind was intensely focused on his rage, but yet deep within his heart flickered a small light of hope; hope that the evil that took his dear Lizzie might see the world as he does and safely return her to where she belonged; hope for reuniting with his family; hope to live with them in a world full of love, happiness, and, well, hope; hope that everyone could feel as he once did. Or if little else, hope for the strength to continue hoping for these things in his new reality of shattered hopes and dreams. This last thought darkened Bill a little further, and the flicker was shrouded once again.

It was late, now. He had been sitting lifeless in the chair for hours and was now ready to get started. Grabbing his bag, Bill left the rotten room behind and walked the length of the hallway toward the emergency exit at the far end of the building. Pausing for a second, he worried about setting off an alarm, but then took his chances on the dilapidated state of the building and shoved the door open. Nothing. Silence.

Bill proceeded out of the back door and walked briskly three blocks north to the old Buick he had bought for a few hundred dollars just yesterday. It was rusted out from countless Ohio winters, but the engine was reliable, and Bill blended in with the other anonymous faces trolling these streets.

He drove around the city for hours. The unusually warm spring air was heavy with humidity, causing Bill's sweaty legs to stick uncomfortably to the vinyl seats. No matter. He was focused: watching, learning, planning. Bill repeated this routine for days, staring into one anonymous face after another. He quickly became aware of the different groups, now easily differentiating the citizens from the hustlers, the prostitutes, the drug addicts and dealers. But Bill was looking for something bigger, more evil. He wanted to hit back in a way that would have a significant impact on the evil people in the world. What he didn't realize was his actions were having a more significant impact on the future of humanity.

Each night, Bill ventured a little further down this tortuous path, eventually leaving the safety of that old Buick and walking among the living dead. Soon, it was as if he were one of them. He moved seamlessly among them, now, and was able to listen in to their thoughtless words and view their mindless actions firsthand. But he learned, and what he learned was that a local pub called "The Hill" was where the apex predators that ran the action on the street spent most of their time.

So he waited, squatting with the others in the filth on the curb just outside, waiting for something, anything to act on. Then it happened, or so he thought. A small group of men hustled by and into the crowded pub. As the door slowly swayed shut, Bill was certain he heard the word *Maven* above the clanking bottles inside the pub and the constant chatter on the street. He turned quickly to catch the eyes of the last guy in, just as the door shut behind him. He was young, probably in his early twenties, but his steely gaze sent a chill down Bill's back. It didn't matter. The time was at hand.

Slowly, unexpectedly, Bill moved from the curb and toward the pub door. He thought quickly about how to work past the resistance he expected to face entering their domain, but to his surprise, the only hostility he encountered was the overwhelming stench of stale beer and vomit mixed with bleach. It was penetrating, and Bill paused briefly to gather himself, then moved quickly toward an empty stool at the end of the bar near the front door.

No one seemed to even notice him enter, no one except the young kid sitting with his crew at a table near the back of the room. He once again flashed his evil gaze directly upon Bill. The Pastor didn't reciprocate and buried his stare into the untouched beer in front of him.

Then suddenly, like a shadow, the kid appeared next to Bill, staring down on him with his piercing black eyes.

"You want something, stranger?" He was cold, pointed, and clearly dangerous.

"I ..." Bill was frozen for a moment, his adrenaline surged, and he actually feared for his life, but rebounded masterfully. "I'm looking for a little girl."

The kid seemed a bit surprised and even relaxed a little as his evil gaze gradually turned into an evil smirk.

"I'm not into all that," he said with the slightest look of disgust as he turned away.

Bill didn't know what to do, but he knew this moment was slipping away. And then the kid changed all of that. He suddenly stopped and turned back to Bill.

"But you know, if you've got the money, I may know someone that is."

Bill stiffened on the stool and slowly turned his own evil gaze toward the kid. The balance of power had shifted momentarily as Bill shoved a wad of cash into his new friend's hand.

"There's plenty more of that if your source is reliable," Bill said, working harder to firm up his control over the moment.

The kid looked at his newfound treasure and smiled.

"No worries," he hissed, mesmerized by his luck. "Maven is always reliable."

Chapter 10

Maven was pleased with himself. Then again, Maven was always pleased with himself. He always had great success poisoning the humanity around him, which always came naturally to him. Modern society, with its high-speed, self-indulgent aptitude, made it just that much easier. Things, by and large, were progressing just as he had planned. All he had left to do now was show just how weak the strongest of humanity could be.

And while the final conflict presented challenges far greater than he had ever approached, Maven had faith in humanity's weakness. He believed with all of his unnatural fiber that one simple act of great adversity was enough to change the trajectory of any single person, and it would be enough to have a great man, of great faith, fall from grace. All he had to do now was prove it. That would be the catalyst he would use to ignite the spiritual famine that would reign for millennia. Greed would prevail over altruism. Vengeance would prevail over love. Desperation would prevail over hope. Denial and rejection would strike faith a mortal blow. It would be a wonderfully sorrowful time on Earth.

And while Maven had not expected Lizzie to be freed from those keeping her for his purpose, it didn't really matter much to him at this point. In fact, Maven even thought that unexpected change of events could work in his favor. But time was running out. If humanity was to fall, he needed to accelerate the cataclysm of events necessary to bring about the downfall. The vernal equinox, the finish line set long ago, was fast approaching, forcing Maven to intensify his efforts with personal involvement. With the world at stake, Maven threw himself into his work like never before. He alone could bring these extraordinarily horrifying events to pass, and he needed to control his own destiny, anyway.

Maven would definitely stick to the plan. He had singled out a simple but extraordinary man. Somehow, Maven needed to ensure that pain and suffering would be too much for Pastor William Binkley to bear, and he was sure the inherent weakness of humanity would take care of the rest. Maven needed Bill to strike another man down with anger and vengeance, and Lizzie still remained his best chance of making that happen.

He knew they were coming. He was ready for them to come. He would use his most developed skills, mendaciousness and deceit, to become a part of their group and destroy them from within.

Yes, Maven was most pleased with himself.

Chapter 11

"Lizzie?"

"Yes, Anna?"

Anna's empathy, fear, anger, and anxiety swirled together, mixing into a lethal mental cocktail. Her heart knew that what she was doing was right, that it was good, but her mind couldn't make sense of the disturbing situation. There were so many questions.

"Lizzie," Anna started again, and the sweet little girl waited quietly for her to go on. "Who were those men? How did you get to that place?"

"I was taken from my home in Ohio," Lizzie responded matter-of-fact.

Anna's fear and anxiety rose. She glanced at Noah, who had turned to face Lizzie and reached out to hold her delicate hand. This little girl was in a great deal of danger, and while Anna was eager to help, in her mind, she was now a target, too.

"How long were you there?"

"I don't know," Lizzie smiled a faint, little smile. "I was moved from place to place at first, then ended up there. It seemed like a very long time."

"And your family," Anna pressed on. "Where are they?"

Lizzie instantly perked up, thinking about her Mom and Dad, but her elation was short lived and was soon replaced with sadness.

"My dad ... he's the reason why they took me away."

Anna immediately misunderstood the child's meaning, confusing the situation in her mind even further.

"And your mother? Where is she?"

"My Mom?" Lizzie smiled brightly. "I love her so much, but she is not able to help us."

Anna turned her focus back to the road. She had no idea what she was doing, but then again, Anna never really knew what she was doing.

"Noah," she turned to him for answers, "what should we do?"

Noah smiled at Lizzie, patted her hand, then turned his attention back to Anna in the front seat.

"Stay the course, Anna, stay the course," he said with a gentle authority. "We must make it to New Orleans."

"Yes," Anna thought to herself. New Orleans. Home. Surely her parents would know what to do. Surely her parents could help her out of this situation."

Anna smiled back at Noah. He could tell she was struggling with the situation, but her expression reassured him, and she was committed to the end.

"New Orleans, it is."

Chapter 12

The next morning, I awoke to find Noah standing outside the barn facing a beautiful sunrise. Without words, we climbed back onto the Harley, and within minutes, we were screaming back down the highway.

No words passed between us for hours as we sped southwest, but now it was time to take care of natural, biological needs. Noah was hungry, and I had to pee. Come to think of it, I was hungry, too, but the pressure pushing against my bladder kept me from thinking of anything but eliminating thirty ounces or so of waste fluid from my body. So we rolled into a QuickTrip just off the highway.

I parked the bike off to the left side of the building. Noah strolled toward the front of the convenience store, then disappeared as the automatic doors slid closed behind him. I hurried into the detached restroom, which was actually one of the cleanest roadside facilities I ever had the displeasure of visiting. I finished quickly, but the relief was lasting. After washing up, I turned my thoughts to hunger, and I hurried into the store to catch up with Noah.

Upon entering the store and quickly surveying my surroundings, I spotted Noah toward the back, staring intently into a microwave oven that was heating some tasty morsels riddled with sodium and a variety of powerful preservatives. Heading toward Noah, I noticed the presence of an intriguing young man behind the counter as I strolled past. I had not consciously paid attention to his being there, but when he threw a smile in my direction, without ever really looking up mind you, never actually making eye contact with me, it made me think momentarily about his past, his present, and his future. Like the very store in which he worked, his job there was a place to stop, but certainly not a destination. After all, no one plans a trip to a convenience store on the side of the highway far from home, much less a job working there.

I quickly cast these thoughts aside as I came upon Noah. He had already visited the soda machine and had filled what looked like a ten-year-old plastic cup with one of the available dark colas. The paint on his cup had all but chipped or faded away, but I could tell it was some old promotional cup, the kind you would get with a "special meal" at your favorite fast food restaurant when the latest blockbuster movie was out. The hotdogs rotated patiently inside the microwave, and two buns sat waiting anxiously for their arrival on an old tin plate that Noah gripped tightly with his formidable hands.

"What's with the cup and plate?" I asked with a little smile as I passed Noah and made my way toward the refrigerator to collect a couple of Yoohoos that would wash down a bag of salty chips and a ready-made cold cut sandwich, which I hoped had not been sitting around for too long. I didn't have the patience to prepare my food, so the risk of eating the old food was well worth it. Noah ignored my condescending remark and remained focused on the task of preparing his own meal. Out of the microwave and onto the buns, plenty of relish, topped with ketchup and mustard.

Clutching my food, I met up with Noah in line. Standing there next to him, I couldn't help but make another crack about his odd choice in dishware.

"So what's up with the ancient cup and plate?" I said gesturing toward his hands. The guy in front of us turned slightly at the comment, and raised his eyebrows when spotting the old tin plate.

Noah turned to me slowly, with his thoughtful, meaningful gaze, and he spoke to me quietly, but certainly loud enough for those around us to hear.

"I choose to rebel against our disposable society, that's all," he said with the most serious tone.

"Right," I said stepping forward.

It was now our turn to pay. But instead of moving along with our transaction, Noah continued the lesson.

"I'm serious. I mean, look at your choices. Your sandwich is sitting on a Styrofoam plate wrapped in plastic. You have two plastic bottles and a bag made of who-knows-what for your potato chips."

My momentary consideration of Noah's point was immediately interrupted by the lady behind us clearing her throat. It was obvious she was urging us to simply move along, but Noah ignored her and continued on.

"It's not just the 220 million tons of garbage we generate each year in this country alone. No, it's the way we have allowed the concept of *disposability* to permeate our lives, eroding our thoughts and ideas, our beliefs and value systems."

For added effect, Noah took a sip of soda from his old promotional cup while tightly gripping his worn tin plate. There were now several people forming a line behind us, waiting to pay for their gas or their snacks or their cigarettes or their whatever. Noah just stared quietly at me waiting for a response, but I was growing uncomfortable with the restless crowd growing behind us.

In an attempt to ease the tension and move us along, I stuck my hand deep into my pocket to fish out the money needed to pay for our meals. Turning to the clerk, I expected he would rescue me from this situation by demanding that we hurry and stop holding up the line. But he was just a kid, thin and tall; his clothes and QuickTrip vest hung loosely on his wiry frame. He stared at us from behind his small, round, wire rim glasses. There was no anger or annoyance in his face, much less a hint of urgency. All I saw there was intrigue, acceptance, and agreement.

"I agree."

Silence enclosed the space between us, slowing down the space-time continuum as I tried to determine who spoke. Finally recognizing that the somewhat squeaky voice came from behind the counter and out of the mouth of the young, awkward clerk, the response had me in a state of confusion.

"Huh?" I replied in an effort to gather myself and orient my thinking toward this gangly kid, whose frame and posture resembled that of an old man, but whose presence somehow suggested an element of significant, if not magnificent, meaning. While slightly bulging and red in the corners, his eyes were wild with life, wide open, and staring intensely back at us.

"I agree," he spoke again. "We have created a disposable society, and it runs much deeper, and spans much further, than utensils and dishware. It permeates society itself."

The line of people behind us had transformed into a small group now. It was only a half dozen people or so, but they were all eager to realize the convenience part of their convenience store experience.

"It began with an innocent pursuit of making mainstream picnic pick-ups easier, more enjoyable, and less stressful for the modern day mother. 'Throwaways' included everything from our cups, cans, bottles, plates, and utensils to the simple table cloths and picnic sheets we relaxed on. And it strikes me with powerful irony that the very group that gave birth to the disposable economy has suffered its most gruesome backlash. We became so accustomed to tossing aside our unwanted things that other items became just as disposable. Small items at first, but ultimately our cars, then our jobs and our homes, and now even our loved ones. Today, our very lives are disposable."

I became unaware of Noah now, the people behind him, the store itself, as the power of this young man's words formed in my mind. The incredible reality of what was happening consumed me. I was transfixed by this kid who had instantly transformed from a young, awkward convenience store clerk into a deep-thinking change agent intent on improving the world through the kind of thoughts and ideas that are not just energizing, but overwhelming. It was happening right before my very eyes, inside a roadside convenience store. I was being thrashed about in an ocean of possibilities, and they were all his.

"I've been working on this theory for some time," he continued as if there were no other thing in the world to do or say. "My dream is to write a book," he continued exuberantly, yet ironically, an expression of regret immediately covered his face as the words not even he believed crossed his lips and were released into the world.

He looked down at the counter and drew a small circle with his finger, then looked back at us.

"Eventually," he added.

This was a strong caveat, recognizing the reality of the role he currently played in the world.

The people were now growing more restless and impatient behind us. And after an eternity of staring at one another, Noah broke the deadlock.

"Well, then," Noah's voice was as reassuring as usual, "You must start today," he said in his disarming and empowering voice.

Time sped up around me as the present moment caught up with the slight lead our exchange had on its usually precise synchronization. Forced back into our current reality, Noah's right hand was extended toward the young man; his left arm hugged his old promotional cup while his left hand clutched the old tin plate.

The kid responded by lifting the swing bar up and passed right through the pressed board counter that had been separating him from his future. Ironically, right then and there, he was tossing this job into the trash can. Or maybe he was pulling himself out of the landfill and empowering himself to do something that mattered. And there was the delicate balance between "disposal" and "empowerment," with the impact on others, both positive and negative, as the determining factor.

The kid followed Noah out of the store without pause, without any perceivable hesitation. No words were spoken. No note was written. No telephone call was made. No acknowledgement whatsoever.

I stood there among the others in a state of mild shock. Turning to the small gathering, I noticed some stared at me, others at Noah and the kid, while others looked questionably at the items in their hands.

"Hey, where are you going?" The lady close to me shouted.

The workman near the back shrugged, moved forward, threw a small wad of cash on the counter, and left. The others followed his actions, some paying, some not paying. I paid.

When I caught up to them outside, they were standing over the brilliant blue Harley gleaming in the Virginia sunshine. The day was certainly in full bloom. I couldn't exactly hear what they were saying as I approached. Ignoring the obvious, I wanted desperately to get on that bike and speed away from this complicated world, to feel the freedom of the road on my face again.

"This is Charlie," Noah said with a smile, and he almost giggled as he said it.

"Nice to meet you," I said, barely even looking in his direction as I mounted the bike and shoved the key into the ignition. "Let's get going," I said, staring directly at Noah.

"Charlie's coming with us," Noah explained.

The impact of that statement was significant, and I resisted the very thought with all of my might. How dare this stranger invade the bond that I had created with … with this other stranger I had met just two days ago. No matter. I had found Noah; he was mine.

Noah and Charlie stared down at me, and I stared back at them. And then it hit me. I had not found Noah. He had found me. He had found us.

Quickly coming to grips with this indisputable fact, my thoughts and attention turned to the incredible machine I had fantasized about since my childhood and was now freely commanding over the open road. Slowly, I looked away from Charlie and Noah and took in the Harley beneath me. Noah sensed the obvious conflict within me.

"There's not a moment to waste," he began, taking a step closer to me. "The race has started. Good perpetuates good, person to person.

And evil does the same. Good must run faster. We must run faster and we must endure to finish first."

I looked up into Noah's face. I felt the truth in his words. Something much bigger than me was happening here, bigger than any of us.

Noah smiled, recognizing my understanding, but also sensing the conflict in me, the powerful humanness that drives us all without proper supervision. And as the thought of what I was going to do with this beautiful bike started to form in my mind, Noah once again showed me the way, turning his eyes toward a man squatting down on the curb near the entrance of the gas station. His arms hugged his knees, which were pressed against his chest, and his head was pressed deep into the space between. He was obviously dejected and currently without direction.

I walked the twenty yards or so over to him and paused until he noticed me. Looking up, his red, teary eyes told a desperate story, but he remained steadfast in his hope for a second chance and maintained a burning desire for redemption. And there I was, standing right in front of him.

Slowly, but deliberately, he held out a hand to me, not really even knowing what he was asking for. I pressed the simple Harley key set into his hand, then watched him stare at it quizzically for a brief moment. His eyes wandered instinctually from the key to the bike that gleamed in the sunshine behind us. He looked back at me to be sure he understood, and I nodded in affirmation. My heart rejoiced as the grizzled man leaped to his feet as his heart leaped at the gift he had been given. Instantly, he threw the blanket of depression and desperation off of him, walked briskly to the bike, and a wave of excitement flowed through him as he roared confidently out of the station and into his future. He was on the road to redemption.

"What now?" I asked, returning to Noah and Charlie.

Charlie walked off ahead of us, Noah next, and I followed. We ended up at the opposite side of the convenience store building next to an old grey Honda Accord that was parked alone. Charlie opened the driver's side door and got in. Without hesitation, Noah entered the passenger side, and I climbed into the back. Within minutes, we were once again headed southwest on Interstate 81, with only the hum of the asphalt beneath us disrupting our silence. After quite some time, Charlie was the first to speak.

"I was originally drawn to the idea by an old story my dad used to read to me when I was young and he was still around," he started as if nothing had happened between the time he first spoke inside the convenience store and now. "It was a Dr. Seuss story about the Lorat."

"The Lorax," Noah said softly.

"Right, the Lorax," Charlie agreed. "Anyway, it was about this character that ..."

Knowing full well what the story of the Lorax was, I paid little attention to Charlie's voice and turned my attention to the old Army surplus knapsack sitting on the seat next to me. I cautiously slid my hand over to the pack so as not to raise the attention of anyone in the front seat. Flipping the top flap to the side, I could see a couple of shirts, a pair of jeans, and some socks stuffed within.

Pushing this simple wardrobe aside, I noticed a stack of worn papers tucked neatly into the side pocket. I was sure my curiosity would go unnoticed as Charlie chattered on and Noah listened with great intensity, so I pulled the papers out of the bag and onto my lap. It was a handwritten manuscript. There was no formal title, just a simple note scrawled on the first page reading "How can we live with commitment, faith, roots, and kindness? Why do we not all strive to be just a little bit better?"

Intrigued, I broke the manuscript open, splitting the entire set of papers in half, then pulling the front half apart again, and I randomly picked a page by running my left index finger into the first quarter of those old, worn pages. I looked up periodically to make sure no one spotted my intrusion, and doing so helped keep the motion sickness from overcoming me. But the words were too powerful for me to resist as I ran my finger down the page.

> ... Marie had been married for nearly twelve years now. She was graced with three children—boys aged ten, eight, and five—all of whom meant nothing less than the world to her. But she always knew something was coming. She could always sense it, like when the pressure in the air drops significantly around you and the cool breeze that sets over the warm, humid afternoon reveals a massive storm sweeping in. And in this case, the afternoon lasted for what seemed a lifetime because the storm had been building for the past twelve years.

> And when it hit, the force of this particular storm against this particular life was unforgiving, and the result was nothing short of catastrophic. Marie's life was now

unrecognizable, nothing but scattered debris, seemingly impossible for one person to recover.

In a simple sentence that included the words, "I really need to find myself," he was able to throw away his job, his home, his wife, and all of his children. And to him, they were piled up nicely in some part of his life that he had decided to leave behind for someone else to pick up. For her, and for the thirty little fingers and toes left behind, that pile was confused, sad, and conflicted—scattered across a wide blast radius.

The story sounded so traumatic to me, so desperate, so awful. But it compelled me to flip toward the back and keep reading.

... but now, in her final moments, she was surrounded by those that mattered. Her boys were now men, married to strong women that were raising their children with a foundation of love, faith, and community. And it was her strength, values, and perseverance invested in years of hope and hard work that paid this mighty dividend.

Marie had made her choices, and they were always effortless for her to make. Sure, those choices were hard to execute, sometimes seemingly impossible to fulfill, but always easy to make. Once discarded and lying among the other pieces of broken hopes and dreams, Marie pulled herself out of the garbage dump and transformed her life and those around her into something meaningful. That was the choice *she* made every day.

Suddenly, feeling like I was betraying Charlie's private thoughts and life, I shoved the pages back down into the bag. I was seeing Charlie a bit differently, now. What I originally perceived as insecurity, I now considered to be more of a quiet confidence that had evolved from a lifetime of thoughtful and selfless choices.

Looking forward, I thought about my own choices. Blessed with a relatively easy upbringing, I had not faced any real adversity in my life. The choices I made had never been focused on helping others; they had always been focused on helping me. In fact, I am sure many of the decisions that helped me had certainly hurt others. Was there a correlation to the amount of adversity in a person's life and the choices to make the right or wrong decisions? My intuition told me that the more adversity one faced, the more we leaned toward making the wrong decisions. But the more I considered this, the more I thought it might be the other way around. I guess the point is that our decisions are ours to make no matter what our situation is. I suppose that's why I, a wealthy, highly-paid and self-absorbed advertising executive, was now in the backseat of an old, grey Honda being driven by a young kid named Charlie.

Shifting slightly, I pulled a bit of nostalgia from out of my back pocket and flipped on my phone momentarily. Damn. Twenty-eight missed calls. My anxiety level rose.

"Where are we headed?" I broke off thoughts about my other life momentarily and intruded on the front seat discussion.

Noah finished his sentence and paused momentarily. He turned to me with his typical deference and said, "New Orleans. We're still headed to New Orleans."

Shaking my head in quiet affirmation, I turned the phone off again and shoved it deep in my pocket. I had no idea where this fantastic journey would carry me, but I was committed to seeing it through to the end.

Chapter 13

Bill sat frozen in his stool as the word *Maven* rang out around him. The very sound of the name sent chills through him, chills that didn't frighten Bill, but urged him to rip the kid's throat out just for uttering the name. Still, Bill remained calm on the outside while his internal rage drove his heart and soul further down the path, where the light that flickered inside could barely even be seen. His steely gaze even unnerved the kid, but only for a moment.

Bill left "The Hill" with instructions to meet his dirty new friend "Skid," as he was known on the street, at the same spot around the same time tomorrow. Reluctantly, Bill pulled the grungy bar door open and stepped into the late night air. This kid was the only chance he may ever get to release the fury that was building inside. Bill was excited. He never dreamed he would have the opportunity to release his fury on Maven directly. Now, that was the only thing he thought might ease his pain. What he didn't know was he would be releasing that fury on the world too. And even if he did know, he probably wouldn't care at this point. But Maven did. He wanted Bill to unleash his anger. He *needed* Bill to wickedly share his pain. And Maven was winning. Nothing mattered more to Bill now than destroying Maven, and if necessary, sharing his pain in the most profane ways along the way.

Bill strolled calmly across the street and found a nook just inside a dark alley where the shadows and a few neighboring night creatures camouflaged his presence. His eyes were affixed on the bar's front door, and his mind was focused. Like a predator lying unobserved in the tall grass, he was stalking his prey, patiently waiting for the moment, his moment, to seize upon the unsuspecting lout that would be his trophy tonight. And wait he did, crouched in the filth for hours; his legs ached with cramps, his mind raced with disturbing thoughts, but he was ready to pounce at any time. Dozens of lost souls poured out of the pub, but the kid had yet to slink back to whatever hole he had crawled out from.

As dawn began to break, the door swung open, and the last remaining demons emerged. As the others dispersed into the early morning mist, Skid paused and looked around, as if his sensitive, flickering tongue could sense the danger lurking somewhere nearby. He looked left down the street, then right down the opposite way. Then for a moment, he seemed to study the alley across the street. Bill felt the kid could see him plainly as if he were standing in the middle of the street, but the recess of the buildings and the trash piled high around him definitely obstructed the kid's view. Shrugging off any sense of vulnerability, Skid headed south away from the pub.

Bill waited for a moment so he would not be seen, then started to stalk his target. He was careful not to follow too closely, but he never lost sight of his prey. Skid was walking at a brisk pace now, darting from one side of the street to other. He never once looked back as he cut west across a park.

Bill's heart was racing, more from the tension than the physical exertion, as sweat poured from his pores and soaked his clothing. He followed Skid down a small path, past a group of homeless people sleeping on benches and tables, and toward the west side of the park. The only thing giving him any comfort whatsoever was the tight grip he had on the 9 mm Glock pistol shoved in his sweatshirt pocket. He thought for sure the kid knew he was being followed, and the thought of having to use his gun now amplified his intensity.

Then, the kid stopped abruptly at the far edge of the park. Bill froze, then crouched down a bit, waiting for his next move. He was easily forty or fifty yards behind but could clearly see Skid up ahead. With a final dash, the kid darted across the street and slithered up the rotting steps of an old, dilapidated colonial house nestled on a street lined with old, dilapidated colonial houses. Bill remained in the shadows at the edge of the park and watched the lout disappear inside.

Once inside, Skid emptied his pockets onto an old, faded bureau, then curled up on the sofa. He turned on the TV, and within minutes rolled over and started to sleep the day away, as he did every day.

He hadn't been asleep long, or so he thought, when he faintly recognized the creak from his floor in the middle of his room. It always creaked when he walked across it just so, but that didn't make any sense to him in his sleep-induced confusion. He was lying on the couch, not walking on the floor. That was his last thought before rushing out of his lethargic state and springing upright on the couch. Instantly, he felt the cold, hard metal of the Glock pistol pressed firmly to his forehead. His eyes darted from the fingers that gripped the handle up to the grimaced face that stared down at him.

"You?" he said in a confused, but somewhat familiar way, as if their profane exchange earlier had created some bond between them.

"Where is he?" Bill pressed the handgun harder into the thug's head.

The kid paused. He looked confused.

"Who?"

Bill's index finger felt heavy on the trigger. He gripped the gun more tightly and even exerted slightly more pressure on the trigger. He wanted revenge, and he was dangerously close to unleashing some of his grief and anger on this kid—right here, right now, as he sat on that old, dirty couch.

"Maven: where is he?"

Skid's expression instantly changed from surprise and concern to outright fear.

"I can't," he stammered, "he'll … he'll kill me."

The irony stunned Bill as he stood with a 9 mm handgun pressed into this kid's forehead.

"I'll kill you right here, right now." It was clear Bill would make good on that promise.

"No. Not like him. He's not natural."

A chill swept through Bill as he took in these words. But the frustration and anger that swirled within him demanded a sacrifice. The pressure building inside was too much, and he was now pressing with more force against the trigger. Bill was surprised the gun had not yet fired. But that was not to be, not now at least.

"You'll beg for death before I'm done with you."

And with that, Bill bluntly slammed the butt of the gun into the kid's forehead knocking him unconscious.

Only threats. The flicker was still there. And while Bill couldn't see the light any longer, he could still feel its presence. A single act threatened to extinguish the light of the world, and Bill just avoided igniting unconditional amoralism by a razor-thin margin.

Time was running out.

Chapter 14

Anna, drained from putting eleven hours and hundreds of miles behind them, desperately needed to stop. While her adrenaline surge had long ago subsided, the constant fear of being caught by whoever those men were, by the police, or by the FBI infiltrated each of her thoughts and actions. Occasionally, she caught a glimpse of the sweet, angelic face in the rearview mirror, which kept her steadfast on the course she knew to be right. It was late now, and Lizzie had been sleeping quietly in the back for some time. Anna suddenly recognized that her own hunger and exhaustion could only pale in comparison to that of the small girl that remained so peaceful throughout the entire ordeal. They had to stop and get something to eat.

They were now in fairly familiar territory, north of New Orleans and just outside of Lake Pontchartrain. Anna approached Covington, a modestly populated exit—small enough to be off the beaten path but large enough to blend in with other tourists and travelers making temporary stops. And this was a temporary stop. Anna had every intention of getting their supplies and getting back on the road as quickly as possible. She had long since figured that Noah didn't have a mother that lived in Louisiana, based on his general lack of knowledge about the state and New Orleans, in particular. Preoccupied with how she would ever reunite Lizzie with her mother, Anna had yet to confront Noah directly. She was certain that somehow he was put on this earth to help her reunite with her own parents.

None of that mattered at the moment. Anna was now trolling Covington's main street for a safe place to stop. She would figure out their immediate next steps, and a larger overall plan, once they had reacquired the camouflage of anonymity driving on the interstate.

Anna rolled the Jetta into the parking lot of a quaint food market that was still open and seemed to be sparsely populated. Anna exited the Jetta quickly, surveying her surroundings. The gravel lot crunched underfoot as she moved around the back of the car to Lizzie's door.

Anna opened the door slowly so as not to frighten the sleeping child. A gentle nudge was all it took for Lizzie's bright eyes to immediately pop open. She instinctually removed the seatbelt constraining her to the back seat and took Anna's hand as she stepped out of the little black car.

Noah had also exited the vehicle and was waiting patiently on the concrete walkway just in front of them. Anna didn't even notice Noah's great smile of admiration and his appreciation for the care she was giving to this little soul as she stepped quickly past him, pulling Lizzie gently by the hand so that she might keep pace with each step. Anna did notice the several iridescent lamps hanging in front of the market that hummed quietly on the otherwise dimly lit porch, particularly when the occasional insect, flying without direction or purpose into the light, was vaporized with a loud *zap*.

For a fleeting instant, Anna felt her destiny change. Like a supernatural shift in space and time, there was something meaningful about her being in this place, at this time. But then she dismissed the nearly subconscious thought as nonsense altogether and concentrated on the task at hand. Getting food and going unnoticed was more important to her right now than any future she could imagine.

Once inside, Anna paused briefly, instinctually pulling Lizzie closer to her as she quickly surveyed their surroundings under the bright, fluorescent lights humming above. It was a rather large store, kind of like a convenience store, grocery store, and gourmet deli all mixed together. It even had a full-service coffee bar toward the back.

As far as Anna could tell, there were only three other people in the store, plus the clerk, which gave her some unexpected relief. In fact, the three men transfixed on the flat screen television mounted near the coffee bar didn't even seem to notice that they had entered the store. Anna proceeded cautiously, but with more confidence, as she worked to remain unnoticed while continuing to study the men.

Anna concentrated first on the man furthest to the right. He was leaning on the coffee bar and facing slightly in her direction, but he remained intensely focused on the television above. His features were easy to see. Anna figured him to be middle aged but was struck by his somewhat odd appearance that she might only describe as a disheveled corporate executive. There was also a young kid sitting on one of the trendy bar stools nearby. Anna noticed his clothes hung loosely on his wiry frame. He, too, stared intently at the television from behind his small, round, wire rim glasses. The third man, in the middle of the other two, had his back turned to her, but Anna noticed that he was fairly animated with his arm around the kid and pointing to the TV at one point, and the next moment happily bear hugging the middle-aged man as if celebrating a great victory that they shared.

Anna was drawn to this man. There was something incredibly familiar about him, something that caused her to move slowly in his direction for a better look. She was getting closer to them now, almost in position to get a good look at his face. Anna briefly looked down to Lizzie, who smiled up at her, still gripping her now clammy palm. And as she turned her attention back to the men, Anna lost her breath, searching for a handle on the moment. It was Noah.

Anna instantly glanced over her shoulder toward the front entrance and thought it impossible that Noah could have entered the market and found a place with these strangers without her noticing. She was even tempted to rush back outside to check and see if he was still outside, but she knew she didn't need to. That was definitely Noah. He was dressed in a slightly different manner, but it was definitely him, and Anna was determined to find out what was going on.

She tugged at Lizzie's hand and headed directly toward the trio. Maybe she had been distracted by her own thoughts and fears or the safety of the little girl she now protected. Or maybe there was a side door that Noah had entered. There was only time to come up with these two explanations for this unexplainable situation before Anna was upon them. Standing just behind them now, she also could see what they were all so transfixed on. It was a local news story that was covering some event that happened in Virginia earlier that day.

"Once again," the news anchor was providing all the details, "as the building burned out of control, Rod Sterling appeared from nowhere riding his 1950 Panhead Harley Chopper, accelerating to nearly thirty miles an hour before crashing into the front entrance and breaking through the barrier of flames that stood between rescuers and the eight people still trapped inside."

"It's infectious," Noah said, smiling and pointing once again toward the TV.

"I'm not sure what came over me." They were now interviewing Rod. "I was given a second chance earlier today, and as I watched this unbelievable set of events unfold in front of me I knew it was my time to act, to do the right thing. So I did."

As the story once again came to a close, Anna's life collided with mine—as lives do along the way—and our separate perspectives became one.

Charlie and I simultaneously felt the presence of Anna and the child, each of us slowly turned our attention away from the TV and toward the puzzled faces that stood directly behind us.

"Noah?" Anna was the first to speak after an awkward moment of silence. Her tone and demeanor were obviously seeking some immediate clarity. "What are you doing?"

Noah smiled broadly. He looked to Charlie, and then he looked to me. Both of us were totally confused, wondering who this person might be. Then he shifted his great gaze back upon Anna and Lizzie as a father looks upon his beloved children.

"Well, Anna," he started, "it's complicated, but without question, *it is good.*" Noah's smile broadened as he emphasized his last phrase.

Stunned and confused, Anna stared blankly at Noah. Charlie and I were just as baffled, but we hung closely to the moment as we had learned to do with Noah. A slight squeeze from Lizzie's hand brought Anna back into the reality of this situation.

Noah once again traded glances with Charlie and me as he prepared to answer more directly. We all leaned in with great anticipation of Noah's next words. With a large, cleansing sigh he started, "Introductions first, explanations in a moment."

I let go of some air with this unexpected pause in the action. I was a little disappointed as he started, but then again, that seemed to be a great place to start. I mean, who were these people that seemingly walked in off the street and confronted Noah as if they were long lost friends?

"Gentlemen," Noah continued, "this is Anna."

Her name was left floating among us momentarily as he reached out and took her right hand in his left.

"And this sweet, wonderful little girl is Lizzie."

Noah gently reached down to the child, taking her left hand in his right as Lizzie continued to clutch Anna's hand, and the three formed a little circle in front of us. They remained silent and still in this embrace for the moment. The child's presence brightened each of us as we stared down upon her angelic face. After a minute, I cleared my throat in an obvious signal for Noah to proceed.

"Of course, of course," Noah broke his grip with both Anna and Lizzie, moving to put an arm around Charlie. "And this young man is Charlie," Noah said triumphantly, pulling the recently-retired convenience store clerk and soon-to-be author closer to him.

Noah let the moment last as long as it was meant to be before turning to me. With a long and thoughtful pause, Noah moved toward me taking, both of my hands into his.

"And this," he said, pausing again with great intensity, staring deeply into my face, "and this is …"

Noah's words were instantly and forever interrupted as a desperate man burst into the store yelling incoherently at the clerk behind the counter. He was holding a gun. It looked like a small, old revolver, but it was definitely a gun, and he pointed it directly at the clerk's head. Now his demands were clear as they rang out for all of us to hear.

"The money, give me all the money or you die right here, right now!" His raspy voice emphasized the desperation that led him here as he shoved a canvas backpack across the counter toward the clerk.

Our small group froze with fear. Lizzie retreated behind Anna, who was now moving slowly away from the gunman and toward the back of the store. Charlie and I followed not far behind.

We watched in fear as the clerk fumbled with the register. She was crying and awkwardly shoving coins and bills into the bag. I had lost track of Noah as we tried to duck low behind the shelves, but I never lost sight of the gunman. Suddenly, Noah came into my frame of vision, which was largely obstructed by the shelves and products in front of me. Noah was moving toward the man, slowly, with his arms outstretched. He was quietly repeating, "It's alright. You don't need to do this. It's alright. You don't want to do this."

Charlie, sensing a climatic event, felt in his heart this was the moment he had been born for. He was prepared to make a great sacrifice for a greater good, and started moving down the aisle between Noah and the gunman.

"Charlie, no," I whispered, frantically waving my hand in an attempt to get him to rejoin us.

Charlie ignored my pleas. He was crouched low to stay unnoticed but continued moving down the aisle between Noah and the gunman.

The crook didn't even seem to notice Noah as he violently grabbed the clerk who had accidentally spread coins and bills all over the counter as she frantically attempted to move them from the cash register into the bag. Then, as Noah got closer, he was now less than fifteen feet away, the man released the clerk and spun his total attention toward Noah and pointed the gun directly at him.

"It's alright. You don't need to do this. It's alright. You don't want to do this," Noah's soothing, altruistic voice continued.

Rage consumed the gunman.

"What?" he said, taking a step or two toward Noah, displaying nothing but utter disgust on his face.

"You don't have any idea what I need or want old man, so you had better just get your face on the floor."

Charlie was now at the end of the aisle, crouching low behind the shelves. Neither the armed robber nor Noah knew he was there.

Noah persisted, moving slowly, but with purpose, toward the gunman.

"No," I whispered as I watched the man's eyes harden and his body stiffen as he pulled the trigger. The sound from the shot was much more subdued than I would have thought. It sounded more like a pop from a cap gun than a blast from a real gun, as I had envisioned it to sound.

At the same moment, Charlie leaped from his position into the air, spreading his entire body in front of Noah as the bullet took flight. The action lasted only a split second. Charlie's body hit the cold linoleum floor hard, and he lay there motionless.

The clerk screamed and sobbed uncontrollably.

"Charlie," I yelled, pushing aside the fear for my own safety and rushing to his side.

The gunman, taking in the reality of what he had just done, turned and fled the store, leaving the backpack stuffed with cash on the counter.

Charlie sat up quickly, which lifted my spirits momentarily, but his concerned expression was focused on Noah and not on himself. Confused, I turned to Noah.

Noah's face was covered with pain. Not physical pain so much, but more like sadness or anguish for the man that just fired a lethal shot. He dropped slowly to his knees, then slumped to one side and fell flat to the floor on his back. My spirit turned desperate once again as the reality formed for me.

Charlie and I rushed to Noah's side. Kneeling over the top of him, his noble face stared up at mine.

"Call 911," I pointed sternly at the clerk who continued to sob as she looked upon the scene.

"Now!" The extra emphasis prompted her to pick up the phone and dial.

My attention was back with Noah. Anna and Lizzie had now joined us by his side. Our grief-stricken faces stared helplessly down at his. He was clearly dying, but his eyes were as full of life and hope as they ever were. I slowly unbuttoned his jacket and gently separated its sides to reveal the gunshot wound in his chest. His condition was clearly expressed on our faces as his blood broadened across his shirt, seeping from the tiny hole that ran from his chest to his heart.

"Noah, we have to get you to a hospital."

"There's little time," he responded unexpectedly and with great strength in his voice.

"Don't!" Anna jumped in. "Save your energy. Help will be here soon."

"Listen to me!" Noah's voice was stern, but comforting. "Don't concern yourself with this. You have more important work ahead of you."

We had no idea what to do as Noah continued to speak to us.

"During our lives, each of us is offered a glimpse of how the world should be. And while it's only a simple, nearly imperceptible instance lost in a lifetime of events, it affords each of us to personally experience the unconditional hope, truth, justice, and love that are the very essence of Him. Yours may come at any time and in any form, like a curiosity we want to ignore, a helping hand we didn't ask for, a flower blooming we never expected. It might come as a conscious moment or feel like a dream or déjà vu or some other sense that is much bigger than we are willing to acknowledge. What's important is each of you paid attention."

Noah ignored our stunned looks and continued with urgency.

"Pay attention!" Noah's demand focused us further on his incredible words. "For each virtue has an opposite potential, and those that choose to ignore His virtues, and by nature Him directly, will release their opposite potential. And the expression of one in the world, good or evil, begets the expression of another just like it. And this is the tension that has shaped humanity for two thousand years. But now the end of the contest is here. One set of virtues was always meant to overcome the other. They were never meant to coexist forever."

As Noah delivered this extraordinary news, space and time morphed around us to reveal a world with two outcomes. Half of the store was transformed into images of a world in which good prevails, the other half was transformed into a world in which evil prevails. Noah himself was now glowing at the epicenter of this unimaginable scene; a brilliant silver-white aura shined brightly throughout him.

Then Noah's body, dying on a dirty linoleum floor just seconds ago, transformed into a translucent figure that rose before us. None of us could make out the brilliant flash of spirit in our presence, but we knew it was good. The images of good and evil started to intertwine and blur together, now spinning violently around us like a tornado. And from within the storm, Noah's voice thundered clearly.

"This is the way it was always meant to be. You are now together. And I am alive within each of you, and because of that there is life everlasting. Lizzie is the key. Just as I chose you, evil has chosen its catalyst to triumph. Reunite her with her family before her father falls. If he does, evil will prevail, and the light will be extinguished forever."

As the scene faded back to the little food market situated in the quaint town of Covington, Louisiana, the group could hear a battery of sirens in the distance. And with a final word, the chaotic scene vanished instantly as Noah's voice rang out a final time.

"Go now!"

I looked down to see Noah lying motionless on the floor as it was before. His eyes were closed, now, but he looked peaceful, even though the life had gone out of him.

Anna broke the moment.

"Let's go," she said and grabbed Lizzie by the hand.

Charlie and I followed them. I shrugged gently in the direction of the clerk who stood, mouth gaping at the scene she just witnessed.

Once outside, we all piled into the Jetta waiting for us nearby. From the front seat next to Anna, I was intensely focused on the sirens drawing nearer and nearer. Anna pulled the car into the modest late night traffic, and we blended in with the few other cars on the road.

"Slow down," I said as Anna sped toward the interstate. Shortly, an ambulance screamed past us in the opposite direction, followed by several local police cars.

Tensions were at a peak inside the little black Jetta, but nobody spoke a word.

"Where do we go now?" Anna broke the silence, expecting an answer from me that I did not have.

"Well?!" Anna pressed, demanding an answer from me.

"I don't have any idea," I shot back. "I'm not even sure what just happened!"

"No idea? No idea?" Anna slammed the steering wheel in unison with each syllable.

And once again, unexpectedly, a calm and gentle breeze blew in from the back seat, calming the storm in front. Lizzie's small voice uttered two words that set in motion the start of the final conflict.

"Columbus, Ohio."

There were no questions. There was no debate. Anna pointed the little black Jetta toward Ohio. That would be our fate.

As we headed north, silence filled the car, fueled by the intensity of each of our individual thoughts. But together, our emotions generated a tangled sensibility. Fear combined with courage and hope, sadness and confusion competed with clarity and direction. While we were inexplicably committed to our actions, we searched for our purpose, our reason to shoulder this unimaginable burden.

Then, suddenly, and to everyone's great surprise, it came from Charlie. He began to recite an old poem by E.E. Cummings, I'm sure it's entitled *I carry your heart with me,* that synchronized our thoughts in the most profound way. We listened intently to Charlie's soothing voice as he prepared us for our greatest moments to come.

> i carry your heart with me (i carry it in
> my heart) i am never without it (anywhere
> i go you go, my dear, and whatever is done
> by only me is your doing, my darling)
> i fear
> no fate (for you are my fate, my sweet) i want
> no world (for beautiful you are my world, my true)
> and it's you are whatever a moon has always meant
> and whatever a sun will always sing is you
>
> here is the deepest secret nobody knows
> (here is the root of the root and the bud of the bud
> and the sky of the sky and a tree called life; which grows
> higher than the soul can hope or mind can hide)
> and this is the wonder that's keeping the stars apart
>
> i carry your heart (i carry it in my heart)

There is an inherent need for love and commitment to one another that keeps the world alive, a sacred bond between each of us that permeates our souls and transcends time, and it's through that very real connection that good and evil travel. Like a network of nerves in your body, it passes from one action to the next, one person to the next, one generation to the next. That is why good must endure over evil. That is how good *will* endure over evil.

We knew what we were fighting for; we only hoped we had the strength to win. Either way, we were willing to sacrifice everything trying.

Chapter 15

His aching, bloodshot eyes opened slowly to the strange and unfamiliar room around him. Blurred by the splitting pain that ran from his forehead down to his left shoulder, Skid tried to focus on where he was. He wanted so badly to lift his hands to the back of his neck in some futile attempt to alleviate the pain, but his wrists were wrapped in duct tape, securely fastened to the arm rests of an old wooden chair. His ankles were in the same condition, wrapped tightly to the legs of the chair. He was immobilized, only able to wriggle slightly, and he moaned quietly from behind the foul-tasting sock that was stuffed tightly into his mouth.

Coming further into the conscious now, he was able to take in more of the rotten, Spartan room from his vantage point in the far corner. An old bureau was pushed against the wall to his left. Heavy, stained curtains hung over the small, dirty window to his right. A single bed was shoved up against the wall in front of him where a shadowy figure sat quietly, masked by the dark shadows of this lonely room.

The figure leaned forward into the small beam of sun that had somehow made it through the dirty window and had worked its way beyond the heavy curtains to become the only light in the room.

"Who are you?" Skid's aching mind now recounted the last moments he could remember, right up to the point the sharp impact of the gun knocked him unconscious.

The recognition in his face told a story of confusion mixed with a slight sense of hope. Of all the people that would like to see him in this position, Skid was surprised to see the man he had briefly encountered for the very first time last night staring frighteningly back at him. Scenarios abounded, but Skid chose to let this scene unfold naturally. He would soon enough find out what this was all about.

Bill gently placed the 9 mm Glock on the bed and rose slowly to his feet. This had been much easier than he had ever imagined. In fact, dragging this young punk back through the park like a drunken, drugged-out loser was the best camouflage Bill could have hoped for. No one even seemed to notice them. The work was hard, dragging the kid's 160-pound frame around, shoving him into the old Buick, and pulling him out. Nothing was more difficult than ascending the flight of stairs, dragging this sack of scum behind him. But still, no one noticed, and the effort was well worth it. Bill was ready to exploit every weakness of his prisoner, even if that meant compromising the very morals he had lived by his entire life.

As he walked the three or four steps it took to be within arm's length of his bound and gagged prey, Bill stooped slightly and stared intensely into the kid's face for several moments.

"I'm going to pull this out of your mouth," he said, extending his left hand to the sock that protruded into the open air, "and the only thing I want coming out of your face is direct and concise answers to my questions."

Bill paused, and pushed his face even closer; his eyes flashed with rage.

"Otherwise, I will end you instantly and move on to the next worthless parasite. No second chances."

Skid looked back into Bill's hardening heart. He clearly meant every deliberate word he spoke.

"You understand me?" Bill made one last attempt to clarify the situation.

The kid instantly shook his head in the affirmative. He was scared. For the first time in his over-indulgent, self-satisfying life, he was facing his own mortality, and he was scared to die.

Bill jerked the sock free, then backed up slowly to the bed and sat down once again. He calmly wrapped the slightly damp sock tightly around his right hand, and then to emphasize the severity of the moment, picked up the Glock in his left. Without ever breaking eye contact, Bill uttered only two words.

"Where's Maven?"

Skid's face intensified, and he automatically started shaking his head.

"I don't know, I swear, I don't even know him, much less where he is."

Bill leaped off the bed and slammed his fist into the middle of the lying mouth that was spewing what he refused to hear. The force of his blow knocked the chair backwards. It remained upright only because the corner of the room caught the fall, and the venomous thug now lay back at nearly a 45-degree angle.

"I only know *of* him."

Skid was now talking in a rapid, panic-stricken voice.

"It would have taken me a day or two just to work through others to even contact him. And even that was a stretch." He was panting, struggling to clearly push his words through the fear and blood that covered his mouth.

Unsatisfied, Bill jerked the chair upright from behind, unraveled the sock and pulled it tightly around the street urchin's neck. His desire to scare this young punk had turned into a desire to hurt him, and his desire to hurt him was frighteningly close to becoming a desire to kill him outright.

With the air being choked out of him, the room once again blurred and faded to black. As his life was being slowly squeezed away, Skid became overwhelmed with an intense curiosity for how he ended up here. The name Skid seemed so ridiculous to him all at once, but not as outlandish as the reality of being strangled to death by a rage-fueled stranger. While he always knew he could end up like this, he foolishly assumed this moment would never come.

And as he plummeted into the darkness, a flood of memories rushed into the black, unconscious pit that occupied his mind, memories like a rebellious condemnation of his caring mother and supportive father fueled solely by his own self-interests. Deeper he fell into the darkness. He was wrapped in renewed and inconsolable grief for driving away his wife and young son, favoring his own needs and total lack of self-discipline over their love. Deeper still he went, alone, joined only by a long string of petty crimes and cons that added up to a lifetime squandered.

He had made his choices, and they were always effortless for him to make. Sure, those choices had great destructive power and often created a great deal of unintended collateral damage, but they were always easy for him to make. Once an essential part of a family and community with a future full of hope, he had managed to ruin his life and the lives that were unfortunate enough to be close to him. That was the choice *he* made every day, and it was his weakness and corrupt values invested in years of indolence and apathy that were now paying this appalling dividend.

But as he fell closer to the bottom of the darkness, something happened. Like a brilliant flash of lightning, he caught a brief glimpse of his wife and son, their faces filled with joy and hope from a happier time that was, or would one day come to be. And then he came face to face with himself, as he once was, as he was originally designed and brought into this world. "David!" he called out his real name in the darkness.

Instantly he was shot back to the conscious living world, staring once again into the rage that was Pastor William Binkley. Bill sat calmly with the slightly damp sock wrapped tightly around his right hand, the Glock pistol in his left.

"Where's Maven?"

The young kid had only an instant, the time it took Bill's simple question to float across the small room, to make a different choice, to change the entire course of his life, to effectively be reborn into a world he knew to be inherently good, and to give millions of lost souls just like him that same opportunity.

He had fallen into the abyss as Skid, a laughable person and existence he had created, and miraculously was once again returned to the world in his original, meaningful form. This transformation couldn't have come at a more critical point in humanity's timeless journey. David, as his parents named him, had another chance, and all he needed now was the slightest bit of inspiration to support a growing urge to do what was right this time.

And there it was, in the form of a photograph on the bed: a picture of a young woman tightly hugging his captor and an angelic little girl squeezed in between them, their genuine smiles amplifying the love and life that flowed from their eyes. Ironically, the young kid's light was now shining brightly while Bill's had all but been extinguished.

"I can help you." The words surprised both of them as they filled the room. "I need to help you."

The two men stared silently at one another.

"You can help me?" Bill broke the silence.

For the first time since Lizzie's abduction, Bill felt the slightest sense of renewed hope. It was deep inside, unperceivable to his rational, angry mind, so he remained guarded, certain this urchin was only lying in an effort to save himself.

"How can you help me?" Bill leaned in, once again emphasizing the severity of the situation, and silently urging the kid to choose his words carefully.

"Listen carefully," David started with a renewed purpose in his voice. "I was with this woman not so long ago. We were together, you know, and she told me about this place she had been. It was an old, abandoned church."

The kid paused, and his eyes never moved off of Bill's face.

"Go on," Bill said forcibly.

"She said it was some sort of ritual, or something. Really weird stuff. And the whole thing was run by a guy named Maven. That's how I first heard about Maven."

Bill stood up slowly. The sock unraveled from his fist and the pistol fell to the floor.

"Ritual? What kind of ritual?"

"I don't know," the kid's eyes opened wider in an innocent, slightly judgmental way. "They dressed in robes and chanted around candles. It doesn't matter. The point is, the purpose of the gathering was to foretell a great event that would change the course of mankind, that a pure soul, a little girl, would be the catalyst for covering the world in darkness, so that indifference and hubris may prevail."

Bill fell to his knees just in front of the answer he had been seeking.

"When? Where? Tell me," he whispered.

The kid paused and took in a deep breath.

"Tell me!" Bill was now desperately grabbing and slapping at the kid's knees.

"I'll tell you, but then you must help me."

Bill was taken aback, and physically retreated some. Rising to his feet, he towered over the young kid now.

"Help you? Help you how?

As he continued to look sincerely into Bill's face, a tear ran down David's cheek.

"Help me be a better person. Help me be a *good* person."

Immediately, Bill started to frantically rip away the tape that was binding the kid's flesh to the old wooden chair. First from his wrists, then his ankles.

"Of course. Of course, I will help you," a modicum of Pastor William Binkley had returned. "Now tell me, where is this supposed to happen? When?"

"The church is outside of Columbus. My friend described a catacomb below. Apparently, no one even knows about it, and Maven makes claims about it being a source of power or something. That's important because Maven, alone, must make these events come to pass. He, alone, must ignite the fall of humanity, and he must do so before the vernal equinox."

Bill knew there was no time to waste. Having studied astronomy throughout his career, Bill knew this annual event was only a day away. He hoped that would give him enough time to set a trap, to free his daughter, and to kill Maven.

"I need details," Bill said, pulling David to the bed and sitting him down. "Tell me everything."

David outlined everything he knew, everything he had seen or heard down to the detail. The detail was so specific, in fact, that Bill suspected David had been there himself, but that didn't matter now.

Satisfied that David had told him all he knew, Bill grabbed the few things he had brought with him. He then turned to the kid with a final question.

"How will I recognize him? How will I know it's Maven?"

"You'll know it's him because he's the only one that knows where it is."

Of course. Bill smiled an angry smile thinking about this simple logic, then turned to leave.

"But he's dangerous, he's evil. You won't be able to defeat him with that," David said, pointing at the gun.

"We'll see about that," Bill responded, then grabbed the door handle to leave.

"Wait," the kid said meekly, moving toward Bill and rubbing his sore wrists. "What about me?"

Bill paused with his hand on the door handle. He turned slowly back toward the kid and said with a powerful, grave voice, "Trust me. I'll find you. If you're lying, I will find you. If you're telling the truth, I will find you."

And with that, Bill fled the rotten room, away from Cincinnati. He raced to save his daughter. He only hoped he would be in time.

Chapter 16

We took turns driving over the twelve hours it took the little black Jetta to transport us from Covington, LA, to just beyond Cincinnati. Barely a word had been spoken since Charlie invoked powerful feelings of love, hope, and determination in us all. Not one of us, not even Lizzie, had any idea what we were supposed to do once we had reached Columbus, but we had spent the last twelve hours thinking about it, and we were determined to get there as fast as we could. Only a couple of hours remained between us and a destiny we had yet to uncover when Anna broke the silence.

"How did you get here?"

Her words were obviously directed at me, but I glanced over my shoulder at Charlie in an attempt to deflect the question to him. But Charlie was asleep, closely nestled next to Lizzie who also slept, or at least feigned sleep, as she was known to do.

Turning back to Anna, I gave the answer we always do when we don't want to think too hard, to work too hard, on any given subject.

"I don't know," I said. Why do we always do that?

I assumed this answer was enough for her, for now, because Anna did not respond for several minutes. Finally, she rephrased her words into an even more difficult question.

"I mean, what motivates you? What drives you to act? What part of *you* brought you here? And be honest."

The question took me back a long, long way into my life. But without examining those thoughts and feelings too closely, I responded with what came to mind first, what I knew best.

"I don't know," there was that phrase again. "but if I look at the last fourteen years of my life, I would have to say money, power, fear, control."

I felt like crying as I heard myself speak the words out loud.

"Yes," Anna responded softly, seemingly recognizing the pain in my slightly cracking voice. "But don't you remember life as a child?"

This question unexpectedly, and immediately, changed the focus of my thoughts, and more surprisingly, took me back to a simpler, happier time in my life, which lifted my spirits.

"When I'm confused, saddened by the desperate pursuit of things I think will make me happy, I remember taking a nap on the couch with my Dad as the football game played on TV in the background. I felt so comfortable, so safe and peaceful in that moment."

I laughed lightly, not because her memory was funny, but because it elicited powerful feelings as my own memories flooded in.

"Or the anticipation of getting a birthday or Christmas present," I built on to Anna's point. "It was really the hopeful expectation of something powerful that made the time special, that made it meaningful. The thrill of the item itself always faded quickly. Within a day, or a week, the excitement over the object was gone, but the feelings of joy and happiness—knowing someone loves you and will be there when you need them—those incredible feelings persist for me even today. That's what I cherish most."

Anna smiled. I once again glanced into the backseat to check on Lizzie, who was smiling, too—smiling broadly, though her eyes remained shut. Charlie was now awake, sitting up and also smiling back at me. There was no telling how long he had been listening in, but long enough to chime in.

"Your wealth lives inside of you," he said quietly, moving his gaze out the window. "I learned that long ago."

Charlie was wise beyond his years.

"But your wealth does not inherently make you happy," he continued. "It's giving it away to others that is most rewarding, creating those feelings and memories for others that don't have them but absolutely deserve them. My relationship with the world—that connection—that is what inspires me most."

I stared straight ahead out the windshield in front of us, watching the road come at us as we moved closer to an unknown destination. "Me, too," I thought to myself. "Me, too." Of course, I was once again reminded about the infinite irony that used to rule my world. My fear of losing the life I loved so much made it impossible for me to enjoy the life I loved so much, but all of that was changing now.

"Well, we've got something new to motivate us all now, don't we?" Anna said, delicately attempting to discuss what we had not spoken about since it happened.

"We sure do," I responded. "But it's unfortunate it took this extraordinary set of events to make me realize what's most important, to remind me to be not what I am, but what I hope to become."

Silence once again settled in the cabin as we thought about this exchange.

"Better late than never," Charlie said.

Somehow, that helped ease the tension of the pending confrontation we surely faced and kept us peaceful as we rolled closer to Columbus.

As we approached the outskirts of the city, an uneasy restlessness abounded, not just inside the tiny car, but outside on the streets. We recognized the usual signs of suburban life: strip malls, fast food restaurants, grocery stores, and movie theaters. And while there were no signs of a mighty battle to come, no signs that might direct us to a final show down with evil, or a place and time to save humanity, people seemed nervous, on edge, like the place was ready to explode. We kept our eyes peeled.

As we rolled through town, my attention was turned to a commotion outside of the local elementary school. A group of young kids, six or seven of them, had surrounded a teenager who was older but couldn't have been sixteen or seventeen himself. Their initial taunts and harassing slaps turned quickly into more violent punches and kicks, and they were now beating him pretty badly.

"Stop the car!" I said forcibly and leaped from the Jetta before Anna could bring it to a complete stop.

As I raced across the school yard to help, I couldn't help but wonder why these young kids, these children, were doing this. Maybe he had messed with the wrong guy, or the wrong girl, or the wrong whatever. Maybe they were just bad kids. It didn't really matter: this was unfair, and he needed my help.

"Back off! Back off!" I yelled, flailing my arms in the air as I approached the group. Less than a hundred feet remained between me and them now.

"Leave him alone!"

And that's all it took, the little kids fled in every direction, leaving the young man lying in the grass, battered and bleeding, curled up hopelessly, being hopeless.

"Here, let me help you," I said pulling him to his feet, and nervously expecting the attackers to return. "Can you stand? Can you walk?"

"Yes, yes. I'm fine. I'm fine," he responded, brushing the grass and dirt off his face and arms.

"Let's get out of here," I said, leading him back toward the car.

Meeting us about halfway, Charlie helped support the limping young man, then asked the obvious question.

"What happened?"

"Oh," came the quick response, "I'm too trusting, I suppose."

I glanced behind us several times, looking for this danger to return, but it never did.

"Those kids approached me selling candy bars," he continued. "They said it was to raise money for a class trip to Washington, DC. But when I got out my wallet to buy one or two, someone grabbed it. The next thing I knew, one of them knocked me to the ground, and the others started beating on me."

"Dang," I said. "What's the world coming to when a group of twelve-year-olds selling candy can do something like this?"

"What, indeed," the young man responded. "This town is going crazy. Crime is up, tension is high. It seems like the place is ready to explode. And it's become pretty hard to distinguish the good guys from the bad guys, anymore."

As we neared the car, Charlie agreed, saying, "Yeah. I once heard someone say, 'More evil is done by good people who don't know they are not good.' It's just too easy to get off track these days, I guess."

The young man paused momentarily as we stood awkwardly at the car. He glanced down through the open doors at Lizzie and Anna, who both remained seated, waiting patiently for us to get in.

"So, you're sure you're okay?" I asked, giving every signal that our time together was drawing to a close.

"Yes, sir. I'm fine. Really. And thank you."

Feeling good about my good deed, I turned my back on the young man and hopped back into the front seat.

Anna turned to me instantly and said, "We can't just leave him here; what if those kids come back?"

I was conflicted and thought about this conundrum for a moment.

"But we have something more important to do," I whispered back at her, confident in my decision.

"Nonsense," Anna scolded me, then leaned toward the back so she could get a better view of the young man through the back door that remained opened. "Can we give you a ride somewhere?" She asked in the most maternal, caring way.

"A ride would be great," the response came quickly, as if the young man was anticipating the invitation.

Charlie shrugged his shoulders and extended his hand in an "after you" kind of way. Following the prompt, the young man slid into the middle seat next to Lizzie, folded his hands neatly into his lap, and waited for Charlie to flop down next to him. Hearing the back door slam, Anna twisted around further and extended her hand out while introducing herself to our new guest.

"I'm Anna," she said innocently.

The kid smiled sweetly; the blood squirted between his perfect teeth, but somehow, it remained charming.

"I'm Maven. My name is Maven," he said softly, gently shaking Anna's hand and turning toward Lizzie, still wearing his charming, bloody smile. It was like getting a letter from a porcupine, but no one in the car knew it.

"Where to?" I cut Anna off, clearly ready to get rid of this kid and get focused once again on our important work.

"Maven," Anna ignored my flagrantly rude attempt to get us moving. "That's a very interesting name."

"Why, thank you," he said most politely, "and just head North here a few miles," he urged, pointing straight ahead, "then left toward downtown."

And that little angel is Lizzie," Anna continued, then turned her eyes to me in the most judgmental way. Assuming Charlie and I had already introduced ourselves, Anna had made her point, but she knew we had to keep moving.

The atmosphere remained tense as we pushed closer to the city. People were gathering on their porches and front yards; concern, even panic, had set in on their faces. The farther we traveled toward downtown, the more people emerged onto the sidewalks, then out into the street itself.

"What's going on?" Anna said, tapping her horn occasionally to urge someone out of our path. Concern was clearly building in her voice.

"Flick the radio on," Charlie made a brilliantly simple suggestion from the back seat. "Maybe we can find out what's happening."

After fooling with the dial for ten or fifteen seconds, I was able to wade through a sea of static to find a channel clearly broadcasting an emergency message. We caught the tail end of the looping sequence.

" … please stay inside your homes."

We listened intently through the pause, and Anna continued to guide the little black Jetta forward. After a moment of silence, the message repeated.

"Ank. Ank. Ank. This is an emergency broadcast message. This message is being broadcast at the request of the Columbus city police. Widespread rioting is taking place in downtown Columbus. Extensive damage and multiple injuries have been reported. The Columbus police are working to restore order. Please stay inside your home."

The mood in the car darkened as we glided unknowingly into a thicker mass of people collecting in the streets. Dozens of people surrounded the car now, and suddenly, someone grabbed Anna's door handle and rattled it violently, then slammed the window with his hand, angry and frustrated that he could not get inside. Others joined in banging on the car and rocking it back in forth. Panic started to fill the cabin.

"Anna, over there," I pointed toward an open side street. "Step on it!"

Anna knew it was now or never, and she couldn't hesitate for an instant. The car lurched forward, knocking a man to the ground and pushing several others aside as the tires squealed forward into the side street. Charlie and I looked back to see a small group giving chase on foot. Anna instinctually sped up, and the tires screeched as she jerked the car to the right, barely avoiding a group of people that had just overturned a parked car. We were back on a larger avenue now. There were flames pouring out of several storefronts on both sides of the street. People were running wild, some trying to flee the chaos, others loaded with stolen goods. Gunshots rang out periodically. Lizzie started to cry as Anna kept the car moving forward.

"We have to get out of here!" Anna yelled above the noise and confusion.

"Turn left here!" Maven shouted.

He leaned forward, pushing his face partially into the front seat space, just over my left shoulder, and commanded the unit like a battle-hardened colonel.

"Right, stay right here. Now, veer left at the fork, veer left here."

The crowds dissipated as Maven guided us down a quiet side street, then into an empty alley. After pulling down the alley about one hundred yards, Anna brought the little black Jetta to a full stop. The alley had come to a dead end. We were trapped.

"Wait here," Maven said and hopped out of the car.

Pulling a set of keys from his pants pocket, Maven proceeded to unlock a large, retractable metal door exposing a crude garage with just enough space to house the little car. He urgently waved us in, so Anna carefully pulled the little Jetta inside.

"This is my apartment," Maven declared as we met him out in the alley. "We should be safe here for awhile."

Maven pulled the garage door down and locked it, then awkwardly hurried over to the fire escape and scampered up the ladder.

Anna looked at me with concern and a hint of desperation. I looked to Charlie for his thoughts. He simply shrugged and followed Maven up the ladder. I helped Lizzie up, then Anna, and then followed the group up myself.

Squeezing through the small, open window, I emerged into the tiny apartment. It was a studio, sparsely furnished and pretty messy. It was way too small for more than one person to live here comfortably.

Maven cleaned some clothes off the little sofa, which was jammed in between the front door and the little window we had just entered through, making room for Anna and Lizzie to sit down. Charlie and I stood near the kitchenette as we took in the meager quarters.

"Do you live here with your parents?" Anna asked the question we were all debating in our own minds.

"No," Maven snapped with a curt little laugh.

"How old are you?" Anna's curiosity surpassed her polite restraint.

"I'm older," Maven said with a troublesome little laugh, "much older than you might think."

The brief exchange was almost immediately interrupted by a commotion out in the hallway. A couple of loud voices and some bumping around turned quickly into a crash, screams, and crying. Before any of us could react to what we heard outside in the hall, the flimsy door to Maven's shoebox apartment smashed open and two large goons pushed their way inside. Instinctually, the thug closest to the sofa grabbed Lizzie who screamed and was now crying. And while Anna tried to help, she was easily restrained by the other.

"Your wallets," the one holding Lizzie said. "Hand over your money."

"We don't have any money," Maven responded defiantly. "Get out."

I couldn't believe what he just said. And his words definitely shocked, then angered, the man, prompting him to produce a small switchblade knife and place it near Lizzie's neck.

"Well, you'd better find some," he sneered, "or the little girl dies."

"I don't think so," Maven said with a ferocity that unnerved even these hardened criminals.

And with that, Maven sprang into action, his movements were so quick and fluid it was hard for me to comprehend. But within seconds, both men were lying incapacitated on the floor, Lizzie and Anna were pushed unharmed toward me and Charlie.

"How did you ..." I started, but was interrupted by more noise coming from the hallway.

Maven shoved the door closed and pulled the little sofa in front of it.

"Let's go. We've got to get out of the city; it's too dangerous here. I know somewhere we can stay tonight," Maven said, disappearing out the little window and back down the fire escape.

"What option do we have?" Charlie pointed out the obvious. "And besides," he said pushing one leg out the window, "I'm glad he's on our team."

Back in the little black Jetta, Maven took charge with intensity.

"I can get us out of here, but you must follow my instructions precisely, without hesitation."

Anna nodded, pulling the car back out of the alley and onto the side street.

"Keep the car moving pretty fast," Maven directed us through the city as the crowds thickened.

"Good, now turn left here."

The chaos on the street was still intense as we crossed town, but no one bothered us at all. Within minutes, Anna had maneuvered us to the outskirts of the city.

"Almost there, take this right," Maven said. "Good. Now stay straight, just keep going straight."

Maven blew out a sigh and fell back into his seat. Anna increased the speed of the car as the people and noise faded behind them. Our fear and panic started to subside, and we were able to think rationally again.

"You saved us," Anna was the first to speak after quite some time.

Maven did not immediately respond, but all eyes were on him.

"The way you handled those men," I started, "how did you do that?"

"I don't know what came over me," Maven started after a long pause. "I just knew I had to act, to protect you from them, to protect us."

"Well, that was something," Charlie said naively.

Several minutes passed in silence, each of us contemplating the situation with different possibilities.

"This might sound crazy," Maven worked to ingratiate himself further, "but I feel close to you, like our being together has a deeper meaning, a yet-to-be-determined purpose. That's why I did what I did. I want you to trust me."

Everyone remained silent. Each of us thought about Noah. No one had any idea how this kid fit into our future, but each of us opened ourselves to the possibility that he was *meant* to be with us.

"Slow down," Maven changed the discussion, which helped influence our moods. "Take this right," he pointed ahead. "We'll stay on this road for eight or nine miles, then we'll head west for another fifteen or twenty miles."

"Where are we going?" Charlie asked the question we all wanted to know.

"I know a place we'll be safe, where we can stay for the night," he responded.

"Where are you taking us?" Lizzie spoke for the first time since arriving in Columbus.

"You'll see," Maven shot back, his charming smile and perfect teeth doing nothing to comfort the little girl.

It wasn't long before we were traveling back through the doldrums of suburbia. As we headed west, the landscape turned quickly to a more tranquil, rural setting. While we remained rattled by our recent experience, our new environment helped comfort us, somewhat. The sun was shining, and the dark smoke from the fires had been replaced with a few white, puffy clouds that floated in the air above. The thick, green foliage stood in stunning contrast to the deep blue sky in the background. We were safe for the moment, but no one let his or her guard down. We were here with a purpose, and I suspected the riot was part of that purpose. We needed to regroup and come up with a plan. I was hoping wherever Maven was taking us allowed us to do just that.

"Slow down," Maven uttered the first words in fifteen minutes. "Our turn, it's coming up on the left, there," he said, pointing to a small gravel drive up ahead.

Anna eased the Jetta toward the tree-lined road and drove slowly up the bumpy drive.

"What is this place?" Charlie asked. "Where are we?"

"You'll see," Maven said with a smile, and motioned forward with his head.

All eyes were transfixed through the windshield straight ahead. One last turn and the drive opened into a broad, grass-covered parking space in front of an old, stone church. Several shade trees huddled around the front and sides while a large, wild grass field unfolded for miles behind it. Anna guided the tired little Jetta close to the entrance, then shut it off altogether.

"Charlie, help Lizzie," Anna said with purpose as she quickly exited and stepped toward the church.

The rest of us followed, albeit at a slightly slower pace.

I caught up with Anna on the front steps, looking up at decades of weather beaten stonework that made up the front façade of the church. Its old pointed gables poked into the blue sky, and two large wooden doors still guarded its entrance.

"This place," she said in a slight whisper, "I've dreamed about this place."

"Come on," Maven said, rushing past us.

He pushed heavily on the right-side door, and the old church reluctantly opened itself to us.

I was mesmerized by the condition inside. The marble underfoot in the front entrance was covered with a few leaves and some dirt but was as solid and pristine as the day it was laid. Each side of the entry was flanked with a curving wooden staircase leading to a spacious balcony above. We could hear birds fluttering in and out, busying themselves with the toils of their life.

We pushed in further under the elegantly formed arches and into the back of the sanctuary. The sun streamed in through the long, broad stained glass windows that lined each side. Thick oak beams formed a trussed vaulted ceiling high above us, stubbornly holding the building solidly in place. The marble flooring gave way to wide-plank pine floors. Clear paths of procession were worn down the middle aisle of the church and between the old, dark walnut pews that were also worn from faithful attendance throughout the years.

You could almost hear the preacher's voice and the choir's song when thinking back to a more prosperous time in the old church's life. There were no movable objects left around; they were most certainly carried off by the clergy or the squatters that followed. But the graceful carvings and inscriptions remained throughout. Complex, intricate symbols of spiritual leadership, love, faith, and a greater time that was or will become.

Maven had made his way to the front of the church and was now up on the altar. I remained with Anna, taking in the incredible scene from further back down the aisle. Charlie explored the vast stain glass images down the left side of the church with Lizzie holding his hand tightly.

"Come on, let me show you," Maven said excitedly as he pushed with all his might on the solid wood pulpit that was erected on the altar.

His pushing with increasing force finally paid off, causing the large, wooden structure to give way, and it slid loudly to the side.

Anna was now more than halfway down the aisle, drawn to Maven and her curiosity for what he had just uncovered. I followed closely behind her, and upon reaching the altar, I stood looking down on what looked like a trapdoor in the floor. Charlie and Lizzie joined us just as Maven grabbed the heavy, iron handle and pulled the door open, exposing a dusty set of stairs leading into the dark space below.

"Come on," Maven said, and he disappeared down the stairs.

"Stay here," I said to the others, nudging Lizzie close to Anna, then followed Maven into the darkness below.

I placed a foot carefully on each step to be sure it could support my weight as I slowly made my way toward the bottom. Halfway down, I could see a faint, flickering light casting shadows on the stone wall below. As I moved closer to the bottom, the light grew stronger, giving me confidence to move more quickly. When my feet hit the dusty dirt floor, I turned the corner to find Maven standing in a wide, open room. There was only ten feet or so of space to my right. Candles I assumed Maven had lit were burning on the ledge of the stone wall that closed in this side of the room. Maven had also lit two broad iron firepots mounted on iron stakes at the far end of the room to my left. How had he done that so quickly?

I couldn't clearly see the boundary across the room, but it looked like another stone wall thirty feet away. The shadows cast onto the stone walls from the candle light and firepots created an eerie but fascinating scene. As my eyes adjusted to the dim light, my confidence and curiosity grew.

"What is this place?" I asked, my voice echoing slightly in the chamber. "How did you …"

Maven immediately recognized my hesitation and soothed me further with additional details about this strange place.

"I believe it was used as a termination point for the Underground Railroad," he started, "a place slaves could stay and prepare for their final journey into freedom."

I nodded in appreciation of the history I was now experiencing directly. It was disarming, and I ventured further into the room.

"It's kind of my home away from home," Maven explained. "I've got food and water," he said, pointing to a case of bottled water and assorted nonperishable food items stacked neatly in the corner. "And a place to sleep," he continued, referencing the single cot outstretched near the supplies.

My intuition had me on guard, but my suspicious thoughts were interrupted by a familiar tone.

"Guys?" Annie's voice ran down the stairs and into the room.

Thoughtlessly, I quickly stepped back to the bottom of the stairs and saw Anna peering down from the third or fourth step.

"It's fine," I said motioning her to come down. "There's food and water. Just be careful coming down the stairs, particularly about halfway down, a couple of the steps are loose."

I turned my attention back to Maven, who was now sitting in one of the three chairs between the large, cast iron firepots he had lit at the far end of the room. As I moved closer to him, I realized the chairs were more like thrones than they were chairs. Sitting up on something like an altar, they were covered with intricately woven fabric on the seats and backs and outlined with ornate gold leaf gilding on the sides. There was a large, wooden table that sat behind them where a number of beautiful, old relics were resting between a pair of large, dripping candles.

I glanced over my shoulder momentarily as Anna, Lizzie, and Charlie flowed down the stairs and into the room, emerging into view from beyond the shadows. Their faces had the same hesitation and slight astonishment mine surely had just moments ago.

"Come," Maven said to regain my attention, standing up and signaling to the table of relics. "Let me show you," the excitement in his voice was rising. "Have you ever seen such amazing things?"

They were amazing. I was amazed.

"Lizzie," Maven hissed, turning his attention to the other three. "Come, sit here," he said, slapping the back of the smallest throne.

Anna instinctually pulled Lizzie close, intuitively protecting the small child from a yet unseen danger.

"Come on," Maven urged them. "You can be the queen, and you the little princess."

Maven's evil grin went unnoticed in the candle lit room.

"It was an Underground Railroad safe house," I called out, still examining the relics and without even turning around.

This eased Anna's mind somewhat, and she moved reluctantly toward the opulent chairs. A little fantasy playtime might just lift Lizzie's spirits, and besides, those chairs were quite comfortable, as Anna would soon realize.

Charlie had gone right to the water and aggressively tore open the plastic-covered case, cracked opened a bottle, and downed the contents into his dry, thirsty body. Halfway into his second bottle, he noticed a thick, wooden chest on the floor. Curious, he pulled the heavy trunk open.

"Hey, look at this!" he exclaimed with excitement, digging through a pile of robes and cloaks he had found folded neatly inside the chest. "There are dozens of them," he said with a childlike enthusiasm.

It wasn't long before Charlie had joined Lizzie's game. Slipping a long, black robe over his head, Charlie walked gracefully toward the "queen" and "princess" at the other end of the room.

"How may I serve you, my ladies?" Charlie said in a terrible Old English accent, kneeling in front of Anna and Lizzie on the thrones.

I didn't care much about their silly game. The ornate goblets, crucifixes, and other religious relics had captured my full attention.

"That is my favorite," Maven had turned his attention back to me, guiding me toward an intricately designed dagger.

I hadn't noticed the knife before, but immediately picked it up to examine it more closely. Two pieces of perpendicular metal had been gracefully fused together, coming to a fine and polished point that glinted in the fire light. The large, golden handle had tarnished over the years but hosted a Cherub on either side, each with a snake protruding out of its mouth and wrapping around the grip, and there was something inscribed down the side, but I couldn't quite make it out in the poorly lit room.

I maneuvered the piece into a couple of different angles but couldn't get the light to reflect the words, so I moved closer to the firepot, raising the dagger slightly above my head and turning the side toward the light. In an instant, the inscription revealed itself to me. I gasped as Maven backed slowly into the shadows.

The moment of clarity hit me like a wall of water. I was looming over Lizzie with this ceremonial dagger, an innocent child sitting at the right hand of Anna in these ornamental thrones. Charlie, in his flowing black robe, knelt before us all.

"You're too late," Maven hissed at me, and his eyes flashed yellow and fangs formed around his thick, forked tongue.

I was frozen with fear but searched my soul for the strength I needed to persevere, to overcome. Evil had infiltrated our sacred bond, and evil was intent on destroying our pursuit of reflecting a more pure existence once and for all.

This was it. Our actions today would shape humanity for millennia to come.

Chapter 17

Pastor Bill found the church easily. It was exactly as the kid had described, its long-lost opulence located just outside of Columbus. The gravel drive, the secret entrance on the southeast corner at the far end of the property: every detail was exact. Bill now knew for sure David had been there himself, and probably more than once.

He stashed the old Buick deep in the thicket, far away from the church itself. It took several minutes to clear away the overgrown brush and vines that covered the secret door carved out of the giant, old oak. Bill pushed mightily on the old door, but it wouldn't budge. He slammed his right shoulder into it a few times, and finally it cracked open. Dust escaped into the fresh air, causing Bill to cough slightly as he waved his hand in front of his face. Another strong shove and Bill had room to squeeze through the opening and into the small tunnel.

Flicking on his flashlight, Bill could only see a hundred feet or so down the narrow, stone-covered corridor. He would have to stoop to make his way, but he would fit uncomfortably through the opening. That didn't matter. Nothing could hold him back now. He checked the Glock and chambered a bullet so he was ready to fire at any instant. Bill was determined to kill Maven at any cost.

He then moved cautiously through the dark, damp, stone tunnel, which narrowed the farther he went. Two hundred feet in, Bill was forced to stoop further, and ultimately, unexpectedly, he was forced to crawl. Constantly pushing the spider webs and sweat away from his face slowed his progress further, but he struggled on through the damp stone passageway.

It took over an hour for him to travel nearly two hundred yards, but he finally reached a small opening, a makeshift portico that opened up in front of yet another arched wooden door. Bill flicked his flashlight off immediately upon seeing the door. The darkness was as immediate as it was infinite. He didn't know who or what awaited him beyond that door, but he certainly didn't want anyone to know he was there.

He strained to listen through the silence, through the darkness, but his heavy breathing sounded to him like a buzz saw running in the quiet night. He focused on calming himself. Closing his eyes, he concentrated, and soon his breathing slowed, his mind focused, and his body steadied. Now he was ready. The time was here, the time was now.

Extending his hands into the absolute darkness, Bill felt his way to the door and pushed his left ear next to it. He sucked in a short breath and held it as he concentrated. His heart pounded inside his chest as he listened intently. Nothing. Bill cupped his hand over the flashlight and flicked it back on, casting enough soft light into the space so he could get a better look at the door. He grabbed the catch handle and moved it easily, which surprised him. He immediately stopped and listened against the door once again. Still nothing.

With more confidence now, Bill pushed on the door, and to his surprise, it opened easily. He pointed the single stream of light deep into the large, dark, open room. The light did little to expose the full view of the chamber, but Bill was able to make out bottled water stacked near his position. He squinted and scooted forward to get a better look at the opulent chairs at the far end of the room. He pushed himself upright and was about to step fully into the room when a rumbling noise above stopped him in his tracks. A faint stream of light entered the left side of the room, exposing a stone staircase leading upward. Then, Bill heard voices.

He flicked off the flashlight and quickly retreated back into the portico, quietly pulling the door shut behind him. Instantly, he regretted that decision. Now he would not be able to peer in on the activity. But he could hear. He heard steps rustling on the dusty stone floor. He maneuvered in frustrating fashion to see something, anything, but could see nothing. Then he heard what sounded like a muffled burst of flame, like lighting charcoals covered with too much lighter fluid. And in an instant, a beacon of light came streaming in through a large crack in the door.

Bill quietly struggled into just the right position. His vision was obstructed, but he could see through this crack into the room. He was first struck by the sight of a young kid, a fresh-faced teenager that looked a bit eerie in the dancing shadows of candle light that filled the room. Strange, but not the powerful, evil presence David had described.

The kid seemed to point toward the large, iron fire pots at the far end of the room, and they immediately ignited, brightening the room further. Suddenly, another man appeared at the bottom of the stairs. This was unexpected. Bill pushed his face closer to the crack, his eye darted from the man to the kid. The two exchanged words, but Bill couldn't hear what they were saying. He wanted to, and he tried, almost willing their words through the door so he knew what was happening.

Bill's mind raced. He retreated away from the crack and further into the portico. "Think," he thought to himself. His heart wanted to burst into that room and fill the air with a fury of gunfire, but his mind convinced him the situation demanded prudence.

And then there were more voices—a woman's voice. Bill crawled back to the door and peered through the crack again. The room was filling up. There was another young kid, a woman, and she was with a small child. Bill's emotions intensified. Was that Lizzie? He strained to get a better look, but their backs were turned to him as they walked toward the opposite end of the room. Bill pressed closer to the crack, wanting, needing to see Lizzie. And as the little girl climbed up onto the smallest chair and spun around facing toward him, Bill's essence exploded with impatience as his little girl stared innocently in his direction.

Bill pulled away from the door for an instant, then returned to the crack to be sure it was Lizzie, to be sure he had not just dreamed it was her. It was definitely her. Bill retreated into the portico once again, giving himself enough room to pull the Glock from his pocket. Rage quickly replaced Bill's happiness, his gratefulness. Vengeance was at hand.

Bill took one last peek through the crack and was horrified to see some sort of priest kneeling before Lizzie, and the older man raising a large knife behind her. Without hesitating further, Bill crashed into the chamber, his life collided with mine—as lives do along the way—and our separate perspectives became one. More importantly, he was pointing a gun directly at me, and he looked like he had every intention of killing me with it.

"Kill her now!" Maven screeched from beyond the shadows.

The confusion overwhelmed me as I tried to comprehend the situation. The strange man that had crashed into the room, Maven's words that crashed into me, it was all designed to have Bill unleash his unfounded fury upon me.

"No," was all I could say, immediately dropping the knife, raising my hands and unconditionally surrendering myself to the gunman, "It's not what it seems."

But Bill's misdirected anger consumed him. With another three or four quick steps, Bill raised the gun. His decision was made: justice would be served, and nothing could stop that now ... nothing but the strength of a little girl's voice through the chaos.

"No, Daddy, don't," she said, instinctually standing up and putting herself between Bill and me. "They saved me."

Bill was immobilized with conflict and confusion. He stared deeply into the sweet, angelic face that was his world and waited for her direction.

"Lizzie's father," I thought to myself. "Of course."

I wanted to help, but the moment was moving too fast for me. Maven, however, acted with purpose. He sprang from his shadowy corner. His face was contorted, and his hair had fallen away to expose a misshapen, horned head. In one swift motion, he knocked me to the ground, grabbed the knife off the floor, and swung it down on Lizzie. But Charlie was there. There was no mistake this time. Without hesitation and with full recognition of what he was there to do, Charlie put himself between Maven and Lizzie. The knife plunged deeply into his chest, and his profound, peaceful eyes stared into the evil that was Maven. Good over evil, that was the choice Charlie made every day, until this day, his final day.

Anna didn't hesitate and took full advantage of Charlie's sacrifice. She grabbed Lizzie and was halfway up the stairs before Charlie slumped to the floor.

Bill and I retreated in fear as Maven exploded with rage. His skin blistered as if it were on fire, leathery wings spread out across his back, and a spiny tail whipped back and forth. His hands were more like claws, now, and as his legs grew in size, his knee joints inverting like those of a horse or giraffe.

"It doesn't matter," Maven hissed at me. "The course is set. You saw it. Your weakness will destroy you all."

Maven crouched low, then exploded upwards, crashing through the rocks, beams and timbers that served as the floor of the church above and the ceiling of the basement below. Bill and I pushed the debris off of us as we looked on in disbelief at the gaping hole that was left. Sun light from outside streamed into the basement. Bill leaped to his feet and raced up the stairs. I followed not far behind. As we burst into the open church, we caught a glimpse of Lizzie and Anna as they exited the front door at the far end. Maven was clearly outside already based on the gaping hole in the church ceiling above.

Bill leaped off the altar and sprinted down the center aisle toward the front door. I followed not far behind. As we burst into the late afternoon sun, a gentle breeze blew across the field as if this were a normal, delightful spring day. But the screech from above instantly reminded us of our extraordinary situation, a scene I wouldn't believe had I not been experiencing it first hand.

Anna and Lizzie had made their way to the little black Jetta. Anna was struggling to get the driver's side door open when Maven crashed to the ground nearby, sending a swell of dust and dirt into the air around us. With an ear-bleeding screech, Maven knocked Anna nearly twenty feet into the brush and thicket, leaving Lizzie standing there alone and defenseless.

Without hesitation, Pastor Bill raced headlong into the battle, ready to sacrifice every part of himself to protect Lizzie from any harm.

"Though I walk through the valley of the shadow of death," he yelled as he launched toward Maven, "I feel no evil, for Thou art with me!"

Bill leaped onto Maven's back, pulling a strong choke hold around the demon's neck. It was enough of a deterrent to drive Maven to his knees momentarily, but not for long. Caught off guard for only a moment, Maven quickly sprang to his feet, flexing his powerful legs this way and that in an effort to throw Bill off his back. He jerked left, then right. He lurched forward, then backward, trying desperately to fling the annoying man off his back. But Bill was relentless. His grip tightened with each attempt to throw him as if he were a professional bull rider on the ride of his life. Suddenly, Maven's large, leathery wings spanned out in their entirety, then launched them backwards into the church's stone façade. Seeing an opening, I raced toward Lizzie and was joined by Anna, who had pulled herself out of the thicket.

"Get in! Get in! Get in!" I yelled, pushing Lizzie through the Jetta door I had just wrenched open. Anna piled in on the other side. As I struggled to get the car started, we watched Maven batter Bill into the stone wall until the beating proved to be too much. Pastor Bill lost his grip, then fell away altogether.

"Daddy!" Lizzie screamed.

With Bill now lying motionless on the ground, Maven blasted high into the sky above us and almost completely out of sight. It only took a split second for me to realize what he was doing.

"Get out! Get out!" I said pushing Lizzie and Anna out of the passenger side door. As we leaped clear of the car, Maven came crashing down on top of the little black Jetta, destroying it and everything inside. We scrambled to our feet and raced back toward Bill as the car caught fire, igniting a series of small explosions.

Reaching Bill, Lizzie leaned over her father, who was recovering slowly from unconsciousness. Anna and I turned to face Maven. I was prepared to sacrifice everything to protect Lizzie from the evil that now raged toward us; my only concern was that it would not be enough to save her. My heart raced, and the fear overwhelmed me. Maven was spewing incoherent, venomous words from his mouth in between the grunts and snorts. Anna was screaming and sobbing but readying herself for the final conflict, her final moments. It was chaos, and I knew we had no way of stopping this beast. Then, through the raging storm around us, a powerfully gentle breeze blew in from behind us.

"Stop," she said. Lizzie pushed past Anna and me and stepped steadfastly toward Maven. The raging demon hesitated; he even seemed to stumble slightly. Maven then regained his focus and charged forward, stooping low to let out a deafening roar directly into Lizzie's face.

Lizzie disregarded the veiled threat and continued with force. "You have no idea how powerful good is … but it is. It makes the sun shine, the breeze blow, a baby laugh, and the birds sing." Her little voice boomed over the guttural grunts and groans. "So much good has happened around me, and for me, even as evil tried to mercilessly destroy our lives. They didn't have to, but they helped me when no one else would. They sacrificed everything when no one else could. But you're too consumed with your own self-interests to see that good things happen all the time, everywhere, and that good things are more powerful then you will ever be."

Maven's torrent subdued; he even staggered backwards a bit as Lizzie continued.

"I'm the opposite of you. I can only see the good they do, the good they can and want to do. Kindness is inherent and it will not be denied, and I believe that makes me stronger than you."

Displaying a grace and humility that only a child could gather, Lizzie moved confidently toward the raging beast, driven and protected by her faith alone.

"Lizzie, no," Bill struggled to speak, pulling himself to his feet. "Stop her," he pleaded with me.

But it was too late, Lizzie raced forward, her little voice carrying forth a greatness Maven never expected. "Good *will* overcome. I am not afraid of you!" She closed her eyes and lunged into one of Maven's powerful legs, wrapping her arms around it as far as they would go, hugging it tightly, hoping providence would come swiftly.

And it did. Maven's leg hardened like concrete, and this effect quickly spread to the rest of his body, up his torso, through his arms and ultimately up over his head. We looked on in amazement as Maven sat frozen like a statue, Lizzie still clinging tightly to his hardened leg. Then, with an anticlimactic *poof,* Maven disintegrated into dust and blew away in the gentle breeze, a breeze that would blow for millennia to come.

Lizzie opened her eyes slowly, her arms still forming a circle around the leg that was no longer there. After an instant, she turned to us and smiled.

"I knew it," she said running to her father and hugging him tightly.

Bill hugged her dearly, sobbing with joy, tears of regret mixed with a renewed sense of faith and commitment.

"Your mother is not going to believe this," he said, breaking the intensity of the moment and bringing an uneasy smile to our faces.

Anna and I helped Bill down the church steps. The four of us made our way into the grass and gravel lot but steered clear of the smoldering Jetta. We looked skyward, expecting a legion of angels to come and carry us away. Or something, anything. But instead, the sun started to set slowly in the western sky, as it did every evening. The warm spring air was a strong reminder of a good life worth living.

"Is it over?" Lizzie's sweet voice broke the silence.

"I don't know, Lizzie," I said. "I don't know."

Chapter 18

We stared in wonder, disbelieving the awesome set of events that just took place. Then our blank stares changed to smiles. Our smiles quickly turned to laughter. Our laughter moved us to tears of joy, and we hugged one another closely. We celebrated life like no other time in our lives. We celebrated good and its powerful ability to consume evil only because we wanted it to. Of course, our outward joy was diminished by our thoughts about the loss of Charlie, but hope had been renewed.

Bill hugged Lizzie tightly, and tears of repentance flowed down his face. I hugged Anna, and a different kind of love flowed between us. And just when we thought our raw emotions could take no more, the universe had one more surprise in store for us. Anna noticed it first, among the laughter and shouts of joy: a car, or truck, was rolling slowly up the gravel drive; the sound of rocks and dirt crackling under the tires was unmistakable.

"What now," Anna said, breaking away from the group and walking toward the old red Chevy truck that was now clearly visible and inching slowly toward us. We couldn't make out the driver through the reflection of trees on the windshield cast by the late afternoon sun.

Anna continued to be drawn toward the truck, but Bill retreated slightly, pushing Lizzie behind him.

"Why don't you take Lizzie inside," I said, motioning to Bill as the truck came to a stop just a short distance from us.

"No need for that," boomed the familiar voice as the door swung open and a big, black boot hit the ground.

"Noah?" Anna whispered as she moved toward the truck. "Noah!" she yelled with excitement as he emerged fully into view.

And so it was. His big smile spread broadly across his face, the half-circle wrinkles in each corner of his mouth slightly obscured by his unkempt beard, his large, pink tongue moistening his lips as though he were preparing to speak. We were brought together once again. And as Noah moved toward us, we were automatically drawn to him. Anna was the first to arrive, and after a great, soothing hug, she pushed away from the old man and asked the question that loomed deeply in each of us.

"Is it over?" Her big, brown eyes searched Noah's voice for the truth.

"Yes, Anna, it's over," he said, gently touching her face with his large, powerful hands. "Good things happened today," he said looking upward and letting out a loud and joyful laugh. "And you," he continued past Anna, and bent to one knee in order to look Lizzie directly in the eyes, "you are the most amazing little girl."

Pastor Bill stepped forward toward Noah; the pain and regret on his face told the whole story.

"Not now, Bill," Noah said, standing up and moving past him. "I have more urgent business to attend to."

I stepped forward, assuming Noah wanted to address me directly. We came face to face, toe to toe, his smile seeming permanently affixed within that big, bushy beard.

"Noah," I started slowly, not having the first idea about where to begin, or even what to say, "your being here is so miraculous for me ... for us," I said, waving my hand toward the others. "I knew you would come for us. I just knew it."

Noah's face grimaced a bit. The big smile was still there, but it was mixed with a little hesitation and some concern. After studying my reaction for a moment, Noah extended his hands toward mine, like he did the very first time we met in Central Park just several days ago. Without thinking, my hands moved toward his. The tips of my fingers, then the fingers themselves, and finally my palms found a comfortable place in his. Time slowed, then stopped altogether as our flesh met, our hands pressed together, our eyes locked. His next words hit me like an oncoming train.

"I'm not here for you," he started. "I'm here for Charlie." The smile returned to his face, but the smile evaporated from mine. "Charlie!" Noah yelled past me. "Let's go!"

I turned around to see Charlie emerge from inside the old church, his boyish grin glowing with life, as if he had just attended Sunday services. He bounced down the steps and nodded with a wink as he passed me and Noah, heading straight for the truck. I watched in disbelief as he climbed into the truck and slammed the old, creaky door behind him.

Noah broke the grip he had on my hands, or I had on his, turned without another word, and started walking toward the truck.

"Noah, wait," I said, desperately searching for deeper meaning. "What about us?"

Noah took another step or two, then stopped altogether. He stood with his back to me, staring at the ground for a moment or two, then spun around with a solemn look on his face.

"What about you?" His serious features amplified his serious words.

Once again, Noah had stunned me with this question. I was stunned.

"What are we supposed to do now?" I said in a frustrated but hopeful way.

Noah smiled broadly and laughed out loud. He took a step toward me, then stopped. He paused, drew in a great breath, then blew his final words back to me, back to all of us.

"You are extraordinary people living in an extraordinary place and time. The thing is, everyone can be just like you, if only they wanted to, if only they would try just a little." Noah kicked the gravel around before continuing. "Your actions will make them want to try. Slowly, over time, others will see the example you have set and desire with all their hearts to follow a similar path. This pattern will repeat itself in the great cycle of life, with generations of individuals recognizing the importance of connection, selflessness, and the harmonious love of humanity, the very essence of our being and the key to our existence. And those that don't contribute to making the collective a direct reflection of a more pure existence, well, they will simply fall away, like a recessive gene being stamped out by enormous selection pressure." Noah winked in Anna's direction. "Maybe there is something to that after all."

Noah looked up. He gazed deeply, thoughtfully, into each of our eyes, then turned to leave once again.

"But Noah," I pursued him further, "what are we supposed to do?"

Noah reached the old red Chevy and jerked the driver's-side door open where he stood before climbing inside.

"Go back to your lives, but live them differently."

I could not conceal my confusion, my disappointment with this outcome. "How can we go back to our lives after all of this? Aren't we meant to do something greater than that?"

Noah's long pause helped to emphasize his disappointment. Then, as if on demand, a strong and soothing breeze once again blew through the trees, prompting Noah to continue.

"Together, we are blessed. That is the only way. Help others see the good that each of you sees. Inject laughter, hope, love, and faith into your days. Shed light where darkness has prospered. Sing where others have remained quiet. Touch those that others have avoided. Lift us up, and show us how to lift others, too. Just demonstrate that we *can* make the world a better place, one person at a time, one simple act of kindness at a time, and the world *will* change for the better. There is nothing greater to do than that."

And with that, Noah climbed back into the truck and slammed the door. I looked on, still stunned, and somewhat frustrated by such a tedious ending to an extraordinary journey that I had yet to fully comprehend. But I was determined to live out Noah's words all of my days, and by the look on their faces, the others were too. And so it was.

As we shared an unspoken covenant, Bill, Lizzie, Anna, and I gathered together near the truck. We waved periodically; otherwise, our arms found their way around whoever was standing close by. The old truck fired to life, and Noah pulled ahead, circling us in order to turn around and head back down the gravel road. As he passed us again on his way out, Noah brought the old red Chevy to a sudden stop. We looked on curiously as he struggled to roll the ancient window down, then popped his head out.

"And no worries," he said with a slightly mischievous grin, "I will be back for you later, when it's your time long from now. And I mean *all* of you," he said, giving Bill a wink as his great smile returned.

And with that, the truck rolled slowly down the gravel path, Noah's joyful laughter faded with the truck through the gently swaying trees.

The four of us stood in front of that old church and enjoyed the cool evening breeze. Our love, hope, and faith covered us in a quiet peacefulness for a long while. It was Pastor Bill who finally broke the moment.

"Let's go home," he said, resting his loving gaze down upon his daughter.

"Home," I said. "That's a great idea."

Chapter 19

My first few days back at work were quite surreal. Of course, there were many, many questions that had to be answered about my absence and whereabouts. And as expected, there were even some that had questioned my commitment to the firm altogether. But all was quickly forgotten with *our* latest win. That's right, *our* pitch was flawless, and it would pay dividends that would be hard to imagine. The third largest do-it-yourself home improvement retailer in the country would become the market leader under our direction and guidance.

But that didn't really matter to me anymore. There I was in the world, living in the exact same place, working at the exact same job, living the exact same life. Everything was the same: my apartment with the Victorian detailing and a kitchen with an impressive ceramic hood over my professional grade stove and range, my plush, leather office chair and the incredible view out the wall of windows I sat in front of, and the blowhard executives that oversaw the hard work of making great advertising. It was all the same, but I was different. In fact, I was a totally different person. My orientation had changed forever.

I now understood the words my father uttered to me that fateful day. "Enjoy the pain of discipline," meaning do the right thing even if it means doing the impossible or at least that which makes you uncomfortable. "Despise the pain of regret," meaning don't look back on your life and wish you had done it differently. Do what's right now, make a small difference each day; it's well within your reach to do so.

Thankfully, I was able to relate my incredible journey with someone that could understand its magnitude, its extraordinary scope and impact. Someone that was there. Anna moved to New York, so we see each other from time to time. In fact, we see one another each night before going to sleep and again each morning when we wake. In fact, we'll be married in New Orleans next spring, and Anna's parents couldn't be happier about being part of her life once again. Who knows? Maybe we'll stay in Louisiana.

Anna has started a not-for-profit of her own for families ripped apart by drugs and alcohol. The kids get the education and mentoring they need, the parents are taught job skills, and whoever needs to get clean and sober gets help. They also learn to rely on each other, to live for one another, and to live for others besides themselves. When it's ready, the family starts a new life together in a new home with new jobs, new schools, and a totally new outlook on who they are and what purpose they serve in this great world of ours.

We see Pastor Bill, Virginia, and Lizzie every now and again. More accurately, we see Pastor Bill, Virginia, Lizzie, and *Colin* every now and again, Colin being the newest addition to the Binkley family. Bill has really returned to his roots and reaffirmed a deep commitment to his faith and discipleship. There is nothing more riveting than listening to his heartfelt passion, earned through pain and redemption he experienced firsthand and imprinted on everything and everyone he comes into contact with.

He made good on his promise, helping that kid in Cleveland get his life together. Bill got him back into school, and David even plays a small-but-growing part in the life of his son. That's just one example in an ocean of deeds of how Bill is making a difference in the world.

I haven't seen or heard from Noah since he drove away in that old red Chevy. None of us have, but I see him in my actions. He made me painfully aware of the infinite irony that the fear of losing this life I loved so much made it impossible for me to enjoy it. Now I'm only concerned about making sure others are happy and fulfilled, which in turn makes me happy and fulfilled. Sure, I still make ads for a living, but I spend most of my days connecting with those around me, understanding their stories, advancing their lives, and supporting their hopes and dreams. I help them to want to try harder, to be better, to lift up those around them, to make the world a better place. And I mean *all* of them. The woman lying in the street, the security guard at the front desk, the waiter at the diner, the blowhard executive in the conference room, the cabbie, the door man, Anna … all of them.

I now see the world as a better place, and I live life for others and not for myself. My life is now totally defined by those I love, and I love you all. Without that, I am a carnivore with cognitive capabilities. So, I open my heart to love. I open my heart to fulfillment. I open my heart to selflessness wherever it may arise. I open my heart to them, and to you. And you can, too. Together, we are blessed.

It's not like the world changed under a brilliant flash of lightning, but I see it changing one good thing at a time. There's no question that it's infectious, and as the good perpetuates and the evil falls away, we come closer and closer to collectively reflecting a more pure existence. I see it changing because I want to see it change, because I'm an active part of making it change. Each night, I close my eyes and fall into a deep and serene sleep with the knowledge that I *made* good things happen today. So can you, if you would just try a little. One day, we might all fall asleep under the comforting fact that good things are all that happened today.

Epilogue

I met Noah only because my eyes were open. The important point, the point with meaning, is that I met Noah, and Noah changed my life, or my life forever changed with Noah. "I" could be "you" if you wanted it to be.

Abandon the need to impress others. There is no perfection: it's just an endless pursuit of self-indulgence. You'll miss a great deal of truth always looking straight ahead. Isolation is certainly not the answer, and exclusion is just another type of isolation.

Take a minute and examine what you spend your precious time, energy, and focus on. Does it make you a better person? Does it help others? Does it make the world a better place, even in the slightest way? What master do you serve? Worries, anxieties, ego, material possessions, power, or fame? Don't choke the inherent purity of good with noise and distraction.

Do good because it is good. Do right because it is right. Love to love. Let's not be what we are but what we hope to become. There is nothing in the world that is preventing us from doing that right now. Your actions today—our collective effort—will shape humanity for millennia to come.

Good things can happen every day if you want them to, if you make them happen; it's simply up to you.

Made in the USA
Lexington, KY
04 September 2012